Shooting

for

Success

Shooting

for

Success

*Your Launchpad for
Skyrocketing to the Top*
Volume 1

Shauna Shapiro Jackson

& Houston Gunn

Author of the Donald Trump endorsed book
Schooled for Success

agency 99
San Francisco, CA

Shooting for Success: Your Launchpad for Skyrocketing to the Top

agency99
San Francisco, CA 94194
http://www.agency99.com

ISBN 978-1-63173-146-4

Printed in the United States of America.

CONTENTS

Acknowledgements .... *x*

Introduction .... *xii*

CHAPTER 1 HOW I GOT BITTEN BY THE REAL
ESTATE BUG 1

CHAPTER 2 ASK AND YOU MAY RECEIVE 8

CHAPTER 3 HOLD THE MAYO 10

CHAPTER 4 A GOAL WITHOUT A DATE IS
JUST A DREAM 16

CHAPTER 5 BOTTOM'S UP 23

CHAPTER 6 DON'T AIM FOR A J.O.B.! 25

CHAPTER 7 INTERVIEW INSIGHTS 27

CHAPTER 8 THE MEETING BEFORE THE MEETING 35

CHAPTER 9 NETWORK, NETWORK, NETWORK 37

CHAPTER 10 FOLLOW UP 46

CHAPTER 11 THE PHONE 51

CHAPTER 12 DRESS FOR SUCCESS 53

CHAPTER 13 THE INTERNET: FRIEND OR FOE? 55

CHAPTER 14 A DOZEN TIPS FOR WORKPLACE CONDUCT 61

CHAPTER 15 LISTEN UP! 64

CHAPTER 16 WHEN YOU WORK FOR YOURSELF YOU
MAKE YOURSELF RICH 68

CHAPTER 17 HEROES 75

CHAPTER 18 WHAT A QUARTER CAN DO FOR YOU! 83

CHAPTER 19 LIGHTS, CAMERA, ACTION! 85

CHAPTER 20 L.O.L. 87

CHAPTER 21 TAKING RISKS 98

ABOUT THE AUTHORS 101

ACKNOWLEDGEMENTS

I want to say a special thank you to my family and friends for all of their support in this journey from a high school teen to an accomplished author and entrepreneur, as well as a spokesperson for youth and future generations about entrepreneurship. To my mom, Michelle, for all of the long hours helping me make decisions and all of the business guidance. To my dad, Greg, for his support. And, of course, to Grandma Linda for always making me smile and sharing her wisdom and real life experiences with me. Thank you to all my "Mentors," those of you who I know and work with, and those of you whom I have not yet met but have looked up to and followed from your books and the Internet. I look forward to meeting you all someday. I hope you all enjoy this book as much as I have enjoyed writing it!

~ Houston Gunn

ACKNOWLEDGEMENTS

This book talks about heroes. My heroes are my parents, Betty and Harry Shapiro. Every success that I have experienced in life can be directly attributed to the upbringing, confidence, and common sense that my parents imparted on me, and I miss them every single day. They guided both my siblings and me toward achieving our every goal and dream. They were wise and insightful and taught us to believe that we could do anything we set our minds to. Most things that I did, and continue to do in my daily life, are to make them and my grandparents, Mary and Louis Goldstein, and Felicia and Herman Zoberman, proud.

My Aunty Esther was the first published author in our family, and I thank her for inspiring me to be an author as well. Thanks, also, to Lori Berthelsen for being that extra set of eyes in editing this book and always being such a great friend.

I want to thank my husband, David, and my children, Drew, Brandon and Riley, for being my rocks. I have been partners with David for almost 25 years, both in business and as parents. Although I learned a lot in school and, especially in law school, David has been one of my greatest teachers in real world application of business principles, and, aside from business, is someone I look up to as an example of an incredible human being. My three children, Drew, Brandon & Riley, have been a pleasure to raise, and I could not be prouder to be their mother. I have always taught them to be leaders and not followers, to be true to themselves, and to reach for the stars.

This book is dedicated with love to all of you.

~ **Shauna Shapiro Jackson**

INTRODUCTION

Hello, I am Houston Gunn, and if you are familiar with my book "Schooled For Success – How I Plan to Graduate High School a Millionaire," then you know that I consider myself an entrepreneur extraordinaire.

I began my journey at a very young age and set my sights extremely high. I am an ambitious person by nature, and my drive and desire to succeed are epic.

I truly believe that YOU, TOO, can put yourself into the mindset that you CAN succeed. That is the first step to actually moving toward success and reaching your goals. The next step, of course, would be to set and date your goals and there are plenty of other tips to follow along the way. This is the first in a series of books that discuss tips for shooting for success.

As the Roman philosopher and imperial advisor Seneca once stated, "Luck is what happens when preparation meets opportunity." So what does that mean exactly? It means that you have to work hard, set goals, find your passion, and constantly keep your eyes open for new opportunities. If you put in enough effort and realize these opportunities, anything is possible.

Enjoy the book, and as I say at the end of each episode in my new web series, "I'm Houston Gunn. Make it a successful day!"

CHAPTER 1

HOW I GOT BITTEN BY
THE REAL ESTATE BUG

A lot of people ask me how I got so interested in real estate at such a young age.

I grew up in the world of real estate. It is four generations deep in my family. My great grandparents were general contractors in Washington State, and they built everything from duplexes to homes. My great grandfather even helped build a large addition to the church they belonged to. My Grandma Linda owned her own insurance agencies and was a successful real estate developer and general contractor who developed commercial strip malls for major corporations. My dad is a general contractor and built numerous spec homes throughout the Pacific Northwest region, and my mom is a real estate consultant, real estate investor, property manager and private moneylender.

So, as you can see, real estate is in my blood.

When I was in the seventh grade, my mom and my grandmother took me to my first real seminar, which was "Trump University." Of course I wanted to go because I got to miss school, but when I got there I listened to every word, loved it and became hooked.

I didn't want to wait until I grew up to buy my first property – I wanted to start right away. So after going to that first seminar, I attended several more, and after about nine months I decided that it was my turn to take action.

When I was younger, I had made some money modeling, and a worldwide commercial that I was fortunate enough to be in ended up paying quite nicely.

As my residual checks were accumulating, I realized that depositing the money into the bank was earning very little additional income. I had been attending real estate and business conferences and knew that my money was not working for me. It was barely making one percent! With the economy in a recession and taking into account inflation, I knew that by the time I grew up, my money would likely not even keep up with the rate of inflation.

I had been watching my parents invest in real estate over the years. My mom would find a property to purchase, my dad would fix it up, and they would sell it for a profit. I started to think that I should invest my money in real estate as well. One night at the dinner table, I boldly asked my parents if I could loan them money for some real estate investments. They thought I was cute, but refused my offer. After thinking about it, they were proud that I identified an opportunity and wanted to act upon that opportunity. They came back to me and proposed that I become a forty-three percent partner on a property that they were about to purchase, fix and flip.

I weighed the risks and the rewards and decided to go for it. My dad spent time and energy remodeling the house and we then put it back on the market. The house sold a few months later and I made a nice profit on my investment.

I was officially bitten by the real estate bug and I wanted more. During this time, I came to an incredible realization. I realized that while my dad was building and remodeling properties and doing all of the heavy lifting, I merely put in money and walked away with a profit. In other words, I made money while going to school, playing music and doing sports, while he made money going to work and getting covered in sawdust, paint and who knows what else. It didn't seem fair, but I have to admit, I liked it (no offense, dad!).

While my dad was out working hard for money, I had my money working hard for me.

Think about this. For all of you out there who might own your home, when is the last time that your banker or moneylender came out and fixed your leaky roof or pulled your weeds? The moneylender typically sits back and collects on his investment. I say, it's better to be the investor and sit in the bank's seat so that I can make money while hanging out with my friends.

So there you have it – that's my real estate story! I can't wait to hear yours.

Houston's Interview with Jay Morrison

HG: "It is with great pleasure that I interview celebrity Real Estate mogul Jay Morrison, otherwise known as 'Mr. Real Estate.' So, Jay, my first questions to you are, how did you get bitten by the real estate bug, and how did you get started?"

JM: "Great, great, great questions, Houston. My story's kind of interesting on how it started for me. I started more so as an investor. I was running around as a young kid -- young adult – and I was doing all the wrong things but trying to figure out where I was going to go next in life. At the same time, my mother was losing her house to a tax lien or a foreclosure. I had a little bit of money and I had a nice fancy car, so I decided to sell my car and actually pay off my mother's foreclosure and her tax lien. She told me she would take care of me for helping her out and I told her it was no big deal. I thought it was the right thing to do as her oldest son. A year after this, in 2004, she sold the house for nearly $100,000 more than what she bought it for. It all started to make sense to me. It all clicked that if my mom, who is not an investor, who is not real estate savvy at all, can buy her first house and make a $100,000 dollar profit in a matter of two years, I

3

knew then that real estate actually made sense. It took some transition time of me learning the industry, but I started in mortgages. I fixed my credit learning how mortgages and credit worked, and then I bought my first property at age 25. I had two more by 26, and I had six by age 27. I made a boatload of money in real estate. I'm now in my mid 30's, but it all started by seeing that real estate makes sense and there's value in owning. From there, I went from investor and mortgage loan officer to a realtor, and then became a builder and rehabber and everything else. So that's how I got started."

HG: "That's a great story! How old were you when you got started?"

JM: "About that time I think I was 24, so 24 is when I got bitten, and I didn't get started right away. It took some time to evaluate my situation, and I was kind of on a dead end road that probably would have ended with me dead or in jail. I decided to make a transition in my lifestyle, and 25 is when I fully committed to the real estate industry and started becoming the Jay Mr. Real Estate that the world has come to know and love."

HG: "That's really great. So how many property transactions have you been involved with either as the buyer, seller, or a realtor?"

JM: "That's a great question. As a buyer, seller, wholesaler, realtor, and even a mortgage banker or loan officer in that equation, I've probably been a part of nearly 200 to 250 transactions since I was 25."

HG: "Can you share with the readers and listeners about your celebrity realtor experience and how you took action to get what and where you wanted in life?"

JM: "Oh absolutely Houston. That experience all started from me making a lot of money in real estate by my mid-twenties and getting into other industries. I opened a restaurant and a lounge and a nightclub and also got into the music industry and just tried a bunch of things before the age of 30. I was very aggressive with my investments. It all came full circle back to real estate again. At age 30, when my real estate license had expired, I renewed my real estate license with a Century 21 brokerage in central New Jersey, but it just didn't feel right. It was a great office with great training, but I knew my purpose and my niche was greater. So what I did was I Googled the richest towns in New Jersey, and Alpine, New Jersey came up. The reason that I did that was because I wanted to sell luxury, high-end real estate. I wanted to sell real estate that I felt was more appealing and sexy and just had more appeal to pop culture. My niche at that time was bridging the gap between real estate and pop culture.

"I think real estate is a really cool thing, but I think it's last on our list as youth and the younger generation in terms of cars and computers and jewelry and sneakers and everything else. I wanted to sell high-end homes. I went and took nine interviews in one day in Alpine, New Jersey, which lead me to the Sotheby International Realty office. After selling myself in an extensive amount of interviews, I became the first African-American male hired by Prominent Properties Sotheby International Realty. I went on in a year's time to bring in our largest listing ever at ten million dollars for a French chateau that I listed in Alpine. I was also featured nearly a dozen times on NBC's 'Open House NYC,' which syndicates globally, and became a real estate expert on the 'Today Show' on NBC as well.

"All those things led into my celebrity realtor status, and then I was able to figure out the proper perspective on branding and leveraging my brand with Sotheby's and NBC. I'm now with Coldwell Banker in their Previews Luxury division. I was able to leverage all those relationships and that experience to court NFL, NBA, and entertainment industry clients. Hence, I was becoming a celebrity on my own platforms, but also was working with exclusive clientele such as professional athletes and celebrities."

HG: "I love how you just started out by taking action to get there."

JM: "Thank you."

HG: "If you could name one word that best describes you what would it be?"

JM: "Resilient."

HG: "That's a great word. Is there anything else you would like to share with the readers and listeners?"

JM: "Well absolutely. I want to share with everyone that real estate is a foundation for wealth building in America. Beyond real estate, in the industry itself, whether investing or if you get involved in the corporate side as a realtor or a mortgage banker, appraiser, or property manager, you can do well. Those things teach you so many valuable and vital skills. Because of my decisions as a youth, I never went to college. I actually was a high school dropout who went back later on to get his diploma. But I was able to become very successful, not only as a real estate mogul, investor and celebrity realtor, but also just as an entrepreneur in other businesses outside of real estate because of the culture and business ethic and work ethic that I learned in real estate.

"Real estate actually was my college. Me, embracing this industry, me embracing the different facets of it, and learning strategic thinking. In real estate, you have to think A through Z. You have to think about your rehab costs, your carrying costs, your costs for the appraiser, your closing fees, and your after repair value. It's so intense. You have to think strategically. I was able to learn those skills from this industry, so that's why I want to encourage anyone to get into this industry. Now I can take those same skills and put them into something like my school uniform collection, Young Minds Can, which is the first ever school uniform collection by a minority fashion label. I'm able to think so strategically, and see the angles in other businesses, because of what I learned in the real estate industry. I want to inspire everyone to not just take real estate at face value, but take it as also a learning tool and mechanism for other areas in life you may want to reach."

HG: "Very true. My final question is, can you share with the readers and listeners where they can go if they want to learn more?"

JM: "Oh yes, the simplest thing to do, even though it sounds kind of cliché, is to just Google Jay Morrison and a million things pop up. You can really look into my whole background. We also have a web platform at JayMorrison.net and I've recently launched the Jay

Morrison Academy where we have a novel course for real estate investors where we teach wholesaling, private money partnerships, buying, selling, and holding. You can go to JayMorrisonAcademy.com, or you also can visit me on most social media like Twitter or Instagram @JayMrRealEstate."

HG: "Thank you for taking your time to share all this great advice with my readers and listeners."

JM: "Thank you. I appreciate you having me. I know you have a busy schedule, and I know you're killing it out there, and I want to congratulate you on your success. I appreciate you giving me the opportunity to share my thoughts."

CHAPTER 2

ASK AND YOU MAY RECEIVE

I believe in the phrase "Ask and you may receive."

Many people don't ask for what they want because they are too afraid of being told no - but a no is better than not knowing at all. If you don't ask, you have zero chance of getting what you want. If you do ask, you might just get a yes.

Let me give you a couple of examples of how asking for what I wanted changed my life!

First, when I was just fourteen years old and a freshman in high school, I had to do what was called a job shadow project where you take a day off from school to go shadow somebody in a field of work that interests you. Most kids shadowed their parents or close family friends, no matter what the field of business they happened to be in.

At first, I thought of shadowing my mom. Her businesses included running a dance studio that she owned, consulting, investing, and private money lending. As impressive as that was, she frequently worked from the house and I had been watching and learning from her my entire life. My thoughts next went to my dad who has a range of experience in the construction world. Although I spent less time watching him do his job, I knew that I was not truly interested in his line of work. I wanted to take it to the next level. I had been to seminars on private money lending and real estate investment, and heard a CEO of a major corporation speak. My mom, being the consummate networker, managed to get his cell phone number after the seminar.

I asked my mom if she would text him or call him for me. She firmly said that she would not. She said that if I wanted to ask him, I would have to do it myself.

I was nervous, but decided that I had nothing to lose. I honestly never expected to get a reply, let alone a yes. So, I took the chance, contacted him, and what do you know? I got a yes! Not only did this yes afford me the day of shadowing with a giant in the industry, but he actually ended up sparking the idea of me writing my first book. I jumped at the challenge and the rest is history.

For those of you wondering "How much bigger can it get?" It got even bigger. When I started writing my book, I wanted to interview some of the most successful entrepreneurs in the world and decided to reach out to Donald Trump. What were the odds? Did I really expect a response? I wasn't sure. But, again, I knew that I had nothing to lose and everything to gain.

I was blown away when Mr. Trump's office called to inform me that Mr. Trump would be pleased to do an interview. And, in addition to the interview, he went even further and ended up giving me an incredible endorsement for my book.

I credit my mom for forcing me to ask for what I wanted by myself, at a young age, and to take the chance of getting a "yes!" She forced me to communicate my wants and pushed me to grow into a confident young adult where I feel comfortable speaking up.

SO REMEMBER: Always ask for what you want. You never know, it just might change your life too!

CHAPTER 3

HOLD THE MAYO

In the professional world, a lot of business deals and professional relationships are created over lunch. I have personally been to over a hundred lunch appointments.

But what happens if you're a picky eater?

Well, I am, and here's what happened to me. For years, I was such a picky eater that my school lunch consisted of peanut butter on white bread only. Every single day. I even pulled off the crust because my mom refused to cut it off for me! If you think I left out the jelly part, you're mistaken. I was too picky an eater to have jelly.

As I got older, I stepped it up just a bit to turkey, cheese, and mustard. But no way would I add lettuce, tomato, or even mayonnaise.

So what was I going to do on a business lunch? I was pretty sure that peanut butter on white bread would not be the daily special.

Here I was at my first business lunch meeting with four executives during my job shadow project. It was when I was shadowing the CEO of a huge national corporation for my school assignment, and I was at a lunch with him, the company C.F.O., the company President and the lead corporate attorney. Lunch was being ordered in the boardroom, and I began to sweat.

In came the order. I saw sandwiches. Good news!

Next, I saw that some of the sandwiches were turkey. Even better news.

But then – oh no – they all had lettuce, tomato, and mayonnaise on them. What was I going to do? No peanut butter to fall back on this time!

Right then and there I made the decision that if I wanted to be in the professional corporate world, I wasn't going to let the lettuce, tomato, and mayo get the best of me.

That is not to say that I will ever be ready for anchovies on my Caesar salad or raw fish at the sushi bar. But I am willing to compromise and expand my taste bud experiences.

Sometimes you just need to suck it up – mayonnaise and all – to socially fit in, and leave a good professional impression with those you may be meeting with over lunch.

SO REMEMBER: They say, "You are what you eat." I don't want to be peanut butter on white bread anymore. I want to be the whole enchilada. How about you?

Houston's Interview with Connie Swarthout

HG: "Please allow me to introduce Connie Swarthout, owner of CJ's Deli in Bonney Lake, Washington. Bonney Lake is my old hometown, and Connie makes one of my favorite sandwiches in the world. She actually has my order memorized. 'Sourdough bread, turkey, cheese, mustard ONLY . . . Right Connie?!' Connie will be sharing some tips on success with small businesses.

"My first question for you Connie, goes with the foregoing chapter 'Hold the Mayo.' In that chapter, I share my story of moving up from peanut butter and white bread to turkey, cheese, and mustard. Then, when I entered the business and professional world, I realized that not having the lettuce, tomato, and mayo began holding me back at a certain point. What ways in your business and being an entrepreneur have you not let the mayo hold you back?"

CS: "Well I think the number one thing is you need to believe in yourself. Many people, because they don't understand who you are as a person, want to give you the downside to owning your own business, and the many problems involved and all the work it takes. I think that doesn't really affect me because I grew up in a self-employed family, and I saw my parents work very hard. I saw them become self-made people. I watched them build their life around their hard work, and I felt that that was something I wanted to do. So I basically just shut all those negative people out of my life. I don't want to say I shut them out, but I just didn't listen to anything they had to say about it. I just knew who I was and what I wanted to do, and I just kept searching for the future."

HG: "My second question for you is, you have been very successful over the years. What are the steps you took to open your own business and then expand to now eventually owning your own building with your business in it?"

CS: "Well, I think the number one thing I was fortunate to have, as you are, is I had really intelligent parents. They were hard working. They weren't rich parents when I was young because they had five children, but my dad and my mom were very like *Rich Dad, Poor Dad.* They were always pushing me and giving me advice on how to go out and learn my trade. When I mentioned to my dad that I wanted to start my own business, he said 'I won't even talk to you until you've gone out and worked in a restaurant for at least six years.' I thought to myself, 'Well gee, that seems like a long time.'

"I went out and really hustled, and I did three or four different jobs that were in the restaurant world, then I studied as hard as I could. When I mean study, I just really paid attention. I watched everything everybody did and how they did it -- weighing out their meats and keeping their costs and the waste down. I just really focused on how I could be successful in that field. Then I opened up my deli! As my dad always told me, overhead kills, so I started out just as a carry out

12

deli. Then I slowly expanded as I could afford it. My dad also said, 'You never rent. You always own your property because that way nobody can ever raise your rent.' What happens a lot of times is that people have had to move their businesses because they didn't own their property and they would be priced out of their rent. The rent would be raised so high that the person couldn't afford it. Well, that can't happen to me. My dad was very influential in making me see the importance of those simple, small things. Yes, you have to sacrifice, and you don't always get to go do a lot of stuff that other people do, but hopefully eventually it's all going to pay off in the long run for me."

HG: "That was a great story with some excellent advice. Now my third question for you is, with all of the business lunches taking place at your deli, what secret things do you observe from the meetings? How are the people dressed? Do they seem to arrive on time? Anything else you've noticed?

CS: "Well, I think being on time is really important. I find that to be very important just with my employees. When I say 8:30, I want you to be there at 8:30, and my girls sometimes even come earlier which is really nice. Just show up. It doesn't mean you have to start work, but just be available to start work if we have to. I see business people come in, and they're always very polite. A lot of times they trade off who is buying lunch for one another, or the person in charge will buy another person lunch, and they always seem very grateful for that. They are usually dressed very well depending on the business, although we do get a wide variety of people. We get construction workers, we get real estate people, it's endless. The city people come in as well, so it depends on their business as far as how they are dressed, but always very appropriate."

HG: "My fourth question for you as a business owner is, what are some ways you take action every day to ensure your continued success?"

CS: "I think your number one key to that is you have to actually love what you do. My dad has also said that you'll never work a day in your life if you love what you do. I think that's valuable because it shows in how you treat people. One really important thing that I think is huge is you have to like people no matter what. I mean you have to really enjoy the diversity of people, and I really enjoy that. I don't usually get too offended by people, because I know I find them just to be characters. I think that's a huge part of our success too, because we do enjoy everybody that comes in. I haven't really had a bad customer. We've had a few problems here and there, but we just fix the problem and then move forward.

"One other thing that I am very adamant about at the deli is that you never say no to the customer. If we can't do it, we'll find someone who can help them. As a result, we just keep growing. Like I said, we first started out with the carry out part, and then we had a response from people wanting us to add tables in there, so then we gradually added a few tables. Then people wanted us to cater, so we started growing our catering. And now we're doing wholesale food for coffee shops and little restaurants that can't have kitchens. So you just have to be constantly growing and wanting to diversify your business. It's constant change and building and growing."

HG: "That's awesome. My fifth question for you is, if you could describe yourself in three words, what would they be?"

CS: "Well you know, I've really thought this over, and I'm not really sure because there's more than three. But I think the most important ones would be: I'm honest, I have a real love for my job, and I love my family. I think all three of those define me, because my business is my family, my kids have all worked for me and everybody that comes in are CJ's family."

HG: "That is a great description and a great story. Is there anything else you wish to share about stepping out of your comfort zone (mayo and all) to take action to get what you want in life?"

CS: "You just have to focus. I do that quite often with myself when I get sideways on stuff. I just have to stop myself and say, 'Stay focused on what you're doing - don't look at the ditch - stay focused on your plan.' Another thing that's really important is taking action to help other people. It makes you feel good, makes you happy, and then it shows in your everyday life. You just have to break through the wall when it comes up and you feel resistance within yourself. You have to remind yourself why you're doing it, and you've got to push past that. Before you know it, it's kind of gone and you're like, 'Wow, that was really cool,' and it feels really good to know you can do that. It's just like what runners do - they push and then they get that sprint of energy. It's the same with running a business.

"The biggest part for me is when I do something wrong and I disappoint a customer. When that happens, I feel like I want to quit, but then they call you back and they understand. Most people are very understanding about problems, as long as you handle them in an appropriate manner and are very sincere about what happened and try to fix the problem to the best of your ability. I think that's valuable."

HG: "My final question for you: Can you please share with the readers and listeners where they can go to learn more?"

CS: "Well you know I love learning. I wasn't really a good student because I didn't enjoy what school had and I feel bad about that. I don't want anybody not to go to school and do their very best, but there are so many other ways to learn. I go to the library at least once a week just because I like to read. I love audio books too. My favorite way to learn is through autobiographies of different people. Sometimes you learn from other peoples' mistakes. That's the best way to not to make a mistake, learning from someone else. I loved *Rich Dad, Poor Dad.* I absolutely loved that book. I thought it was an easy read and I learned a lot from it. I've read your book, which is awesome. You've done a great job with that, and I can hardly wait to read your next book. I just think it's really important to remember that everybody's different. That's what I've learned from the different reading I've done, just as you're doing well at what you believe is valuable, other people are doing other things that are valuable to them. You have to follow what your passion is, not someone else's passion. I think that's valuable. And of course if you're in the Western Washington area, stop by CJ's Deli, and pick up a sandwich and your book that we are selling here!"

HG: "Tell them Houston sent you! Thanks, Connie, for taking time out of your day to share all of this great advice."

CHAPTER 4

A GOAL WITHOUT A DATE
IS JUST A DREAM

It is extremely important to set a target date for your goal, because, as I like to say, a goal without a date is just a dream.

First, set a realistic time frame to accomplish your goal. Make sure you give yourself enough time, but not too much time so that you don't procrastinate.

Second, if your goal requires several steps, divide that goal into separate time frames. For example, you may want to accomplish a certain task by April, another by May and then strive to reach your ultimate goal by June.

Third, always visualize your end goal as if it is part of your reality. Believe that you will make it happen.

Give yourself a daily reminder of your goal. Write it down and put your note in a prominent place such as on your refrigerator door, computer screen, or bathroom mirror. This will give you a constant reminder of what you are trying to accomplish.

In addition to my many business goals, I set a fun goal of getting myself a blue Corvette by a certain date. I put a photo of a blue Corvette up on my bedroom wall so that I was reminded to work toward my goal every single time I walked into that room. So, did I get my Corvette? I'll bet you can guess the answer to that! Check out my web series to see the details!

It is always great to get someone on board who will hold you accountable in connection with reaching your goal. A person who is on your side, who has your best interest at heart and wants to see you succeed. If you are only accountable to yourself, it's very easy to blow off your goal until "tomorrow." If someone is encouraging you and keeping you on track, this accountability partner will help you succeed.

If you believe that you need something from someone else to get you closer to your goal, remember to always ask! Just as I outlined in the second chapter of this book, "Ask and You May Receive," you have absolutely nothing to lose. If you do not get a response or you get a "no," you have lost nothing. If, alternatively, you get a "yes," then you have scored!

If for some reason you don't reach your goal by your set date, don't give up. See what you did or didn't do, learn from it, and then decide what you can do better. Set a new date and go for it!

SO REMEMBER: Set your goal, date it, and do it.

Houston's Interview with David T. Fagan

HG: "My special guest is marketing and public relations guru, David T. Fagan. David is the former CEO of Guerrilla Marketing and previous owner of Levine Communications Office, a Beverly Hills Public Relations firm that has represented 34 Grammy Winners, 44 New York Times Best Sellers, 58 Academy Award Winners, and INC 500 companies. Some previous clients include motivational speaker Brian Tracy, Jump Jet, a private jet company, and Paul Stanley from the band KISS. David is the current owner of Icon Builder Media, and he will be sharing the importance of goals versus dreams. So David, my first question for you is, how important do you think goals are for achieving success?"

DF: "Well they're really important, but I look at goals a lot differently than most people. As a matter a fact, I'll probably kind of blow your mind a little bit because I really don't believe in long-term goals. Of course, there is always some kind of exception to the rule, but I really believe in more short term power plays. What is something that you can do in the next four to eight weeks that is going to get you major results or make you good money? There are a lot of things that I have done in my life that have proved to be really positive, but I didn't really set out to do them. It's important to be somewhat of an opportunist.

"We want to set goals about things we want to do in the short term, but I am not a big believer in long term goals. That kind of blows people away. They will say, 'Where are you going to be in five years or where are you going to be in three years?' I honestly don't know. I know that it's going to be doing something I love, and I'm passionate about a lot of different things, but I'm always looking at what's going to pay me the most money for my core competency, for my talents in marketing, PR, and in transformations."

HG: "That is some excellent advice. Now my second question for you is, David, is there any advice you have when it comes to setting goals?"

DF: "Well sure, and I say this all the time. 'Dreaming is good, but doing is better.' We've got to be doers.

"It's interesting -- quitting is kind of the secret art of winning. You hear a lot of people say, 'Quitters never win; you can't quit.' But sometimes you have to. The trick is, when you commit to something or you take action on something, you want to set a time frame. You want to make sure you don't quit or give up within that time frame. We always need to be reevaluating things, so if you're going to try something new or you're going to try something bold, give it three months, give it six months, or give it a year. Then really evaluate it. You have got to do that because if you don't, you can have a bad day, you can have a bad week, you can have a bad month, and you can throw in the towel too early. So yes, you don't want to quit in the general long term, but in smaller ways and smaller times you do.

"For example, look at Oprah. She was on the radio, and she quit to go to television. Michael Jordan was in baseball, but he quit to go back to basketball. There are all kinds of stories about people who quit things. Ellen DeGeneres, she kind of quit acting. She did okay, but she kind of ran into a wall and wasn't going anywhere, so she went and took a talk show. Some people might say, 'Oh look, they quit; they're quitters,' but we don't think of them as quitters. We think of them as really successful people because they tried really hard, they did it for a certain period of time, they analyzed it, they tried other things, and they experimented. We've got to be somewhat of a mad scientist when it comes to business."

HG: "That's great. Now my third question for you: What should people do if they don't achieve their goals by their intended date?"

DF: "Well they need to evaluate it, they need to look and see if anything will be different in the next period of time. So let's say you set a goal; you want to make X number of dollars in six months. If you get to six months and haven't made that money, then you need to reevaluate and determine if something will be different in the next six months. In other words, did you do a lot of setup? Did you have a lot of things you needed to learn? Do you have a lot of things that are really close to moving forward such as new clients that are getting ready to sign on, new projects that are coming to fruition? So the big question is, will anything be different in the next three months, the next six months, or the next year? That's tricky because sometimes we just want to keep going and keep going and keep going. We've had it forced into our heads that we've got to keep going. Quitters never win, but there are times when we need to realize that we're better someplace else. So reevaluate it, look at it, and really see if something is going to be different in the next set time frame. If there really isn't going to be a difference in the market place or in your business, then I think that's where you start looking for the next big thing for yourself and you start looking to reinvent yourself."

HG: "That's excellent. And now my fourth question for you: If you could describe yourself in three words what would those words be?"

DF: "'Inspire, create, perform.' Those are my three words. I love to inspire people. I try to live my life in a way that I can receive a lot of inspiration. I believe all of the best things and the best answers come through inspiration, so I want to be inspired, I want to help other people be inspired, and I'm very passionate about that.

"The next one is to create, I believe that we are all born creators here in this life. Some of us create food, some of us create houses, some of us create businesses, some of us create art, some of us create music, and the list goes on and on. I love to help people create, I love to help people transform, and I love to create myself. I love to write books, I love to create videos, and I think there's all these ways that I can create things that will make the business world, and the world in general, a better place. I'm always excited when I get to sit back and see anything that I have created.

"The third one is performance. I think we all want to perform well. I'm always looking for ways to reach a higher level of performance and, again, I want to help other people reach a higher level of performance. I'm always looking at music that I listen to that might inspire me or help me create and maybe perform at a higher level. I look to see if there is a certain kind of working environment, are there certain kinds of ways of going about things, business best practices, what different successful people do to solve problems and overcome challenges. I want to follow those things and learn from those things so that I can perform at the highest level and help other people perform at the highest level. Again, I believe it's inspiration, creation, performance."

HG: "That's awesome. My fifth question for you is, when did you start turning dreams into goals?"

DF: "That's a really good question. I think we all do it even just as kids if you play sports, if you play an instrument, you go to school and get good grades. I think early on there's all kinds of goals, but those are mostly goals that school, parents, and the world impose upon us. But as far as my own goals, I did it pretty early on. At seventeen, I was doing sales, and I saw people making really good money. I started giving myself daily and weekly goals to try to learn from them and do what they were doing and not try to reinvent the wheel but have success mirror success. I think it was my first sales job at an electronics company called *The Good Guys* back when computers and cell phones were really starting to take off. It sounds kind of funny to say! That actually makes me feel a little bit older.

"That's what I was on the cutting edge of. I was in the right place at the right time and I really wanted to do well. I've always been kind of competitive with myself, I've always wanted to push myself, I've always wanted to be one of the best. So I think that's really when I first started setting goals for myself such as, 'Okay, I need to have so many conversations; I need to talk to so many people.' You kind of learn that a lot of sales and business is just arithmetic. It's all about the number of people we can talk to and proposals and objections we can handle. I started thinking a lot about that and setting goals. 'If I am going to help this many people, then I've got to talk to this many people . . . and if I talk to this many people, then I am going to have to work this many hours and this many days.' Yes, it was pretty early on. I think I had some good mentors, and that helped me in a huge way."

HG: "That's amazing! Now my next question for you is, is there anything else you would like to share with the readers and listeners about goals?"

DF: "I think again you need to challenge the status quo. I think it's great to think in general about where you want to be 3, 5, or maybe 10 years out. However, I'd really encourage you to just think about where you want to be at the end of the week? Where do you want to be in a month? How are you going to measure your successes over short periods of time? I think by measuring things in short periods of time, you're going to know if you are on track for BIG successful things to happen for you. I think that is really important. It is about mastering the moments. If you can master the moments and the minutes, the days start to take care of themselves, the weeks start to take care of themselves, and so on and so forth. Really just break it down to, 'What do I have to do right now?' We are kind of quick to say we are going to start tomorrow or we are going to start next week. 'This month is shot, so let's just start next month, and jeez, what a terrible year, let's just start next year.' We cannot put it off. You need to go right now and do something that will make a difference. Be quantifiable, make it measureable, track it, and inventory it. That is the most important thing you can do."

HG: "I absolutely agree. Now my final question for you is, where can people go if they want to learn more?"

DF: "They can go to DavidTFagan.com. That's my main site, and it's kind of got a portal to some of my other sites. On that site you will see lots of things about inspiration, creation, and performance. If you're a business owner and you're looking to grow your brand, you want to get better sales conversions, you want to get in the media, maybe you want to write a book, and maybe you want a better website, then you want to look at iconbuildermedia.com. Icon Builder Media is my main company, and we do everything from PR to magazines to websites and books. You name it, we pretty much do it when it comes to building successful brands and businesses. So if you have a business and you want to see what we do there, go to iconbuildermedia.com and maybe that is the way to go."

HG: "Thank you for taking the time to share some excellent advice about setting goals."

DF: "No problem, it's been an honor. Thank you so much for having me on."

CHAPTER 5

BOTTOM'S UP

A lot of people graduate college with a degree, and then expect to make a large sum of money at their dream job right off the bat. Well, it doesn't always work that way. In fact, it's highly unlikely.

There are millions of college graduates that are unemployed. When you graduate, do not have an entitled attitude where you feel that you must make a certain salary right out of school and, likewise, don't think you are entitled to a certain job title right off the bat. Start at the bottom if you have to. Prove yourself, make yourself irreplaceable, and be willing to work your way up. Do not worry about salary at the beginning. Once you've proven yourself, your price tag will then follow.

If you decide to start a business like I have, it is also important to learn everything about your industry from the bottom up. Not only do you want to learn everything at your company, but you want to learn what your competitors are doing as well. Just like building a house, your business must be built on a strong foundation – and that foundation is YOU.

It is also important to do a self-skill assessment. First, figure out which skills you already have that you can use to contribute to the business you are trying to build. Second, figure out what other skills are needed to thrive in that business. Third, fill the gap by either learning the areas that you don't know, or employing or partnering with other people who can fill that gap.

SO REMEMBER: Don't be afraid of hard work and working from the bottom up!

CHAPTER 6

DON'T AIM FOR A J.O.B.!

Do you know what J.O.B. stands for? It means, "Just over broke!"

I don't want a J.O.B. – do you?!

I decided early on that I wanted to figure out what I really enjoy doing and then find a way to make money at it. If you get paid for your passion, then you'll never work a day in your life. At the same time, you need to consider the kind of life you want to set up for yourself. If you enjoy eating nachos on the couch, that isn't going to get you very far in life. The operative words are "finding a way to make money in an area that you enjoy so that you may be able to live the kind of life you aspire to live."

I love real estate, writing and music so I am finding multiple ways to monetize those interests. For me, I want to be my own boss and not worry about cutbacks, layoffs or clocking in. Yes, being an entrepreneur means that I would have more responsibility and in some cases, less job security, but I would rather try to make money my way, and be in control of my own destiny, for better or for worse.

For those of you who aren't exactly sure what you're passionate about, think about what you love to do in your down time.

Do you love cooking? Open a great restaurant.

Do you like working in the yard? Become a landscape architect.

Do you like to write? Write a book.

If you want to get into a profession that requires a professional degree, work hard in school, go to college and then pursue that profession.

You get the picture.

When you wake up every morning to go to work and you are about to embark on something you like to do, it often doesn't feel like work at all! The more you like what you do, the better you are at it.

Once you figure out an area that you enjoy or are good at, try to think of a unique angle and find a niche so that you and your business, product or service can stand out in today's marketplace. Even if you are in a profession you love, try not to fall into a boring routine. You will likely be happiest if you continually challenge yourself, learn, and grow in your profession or field of work.

SO REMEMBER: Think about what you enjoy doing most, write down your top 5, and then think of ways that you can get paid for it!

CHAPTER 7

INTERVIEW INSIGHTS

You are about to go on an interview and you have the jitters. You want to do well and stand out from the competition. But how?

First, I suggest that you do research online to know everything you can about the person or the company you will be meeting with. Most companies have websites, so that is a great place to start. Browse the website and then check out other sites or articles that your search engine may bring up about the person or company.

You should also look to see if the company has a page on Facebook or is on Twitter. Check out recent posts to give you some insight about the company culture. You would be amazed at how much information is at your fingertips!

I recently learned of a website called Glassdoor which was apparently set up to give anonymous company reviews and lots of company information including salary information. They also have an interview section where people post questions that they were asked on their interviews for different positions at that company. So, you may want to check to see if the company you are interviewing for is on Glassdoor!

Next, see if any of your close friends or family know anyone who works at the company, and, if so, perhaps they would put in a good word for you? If you want to see who works at the company, you will typically be able to get that information on the company website or on websites such as LinkedIn.

Next, always go to the interview prepared to ask an intelligent question or two about the company that is not easily found online. This shows the interviewer that you have done your homework, and are truly interested in them.

If you have never interviewed before, some experts feel it is a good idea to do some practice interviews at places where you don't necessarily want to land the position. Get the feel for it. The more practice you have, the more comfortable you will become. Then go to the interview for your dream job.

On the day of your interview, make sure you dress for success and look well put together.

Arrive early, taking into account potential traffic and consider yourself "in" the "interview," conducting yourself in a professional manner, from the moment you arrive in the parking lot until the moment you drive away.

Greet the receptionist and others you encounter warmly.

During the interview, be friendly and confident. Look your interviewer in the eye, and greet them with a smile and a firm handshake. Further, although this may go without saying, turn your phone to silent during the interview. The last thing you want is for your phone to ring, especially if you have a questionable ringtone!

If the interviewer asks you a question that throws you, don't feel pressured to answer quickly or say the first thing that comes to your mind. You can take a moment and say something like "Let me think about that for a second" to give you a moment to gather your thoughts.

And once the interview is over, make sure to send them a handwritten thank you note. That extra touch tends to go a long way.

SO REMEMBER: Do you research, conduct yourself professionally at all times and practice interviewing. Then go out there and try to land your dream job.

Houston's Interview with Dana Manciagli

HG: "I have a special guest that would like to share their insights about interviewing. With me is Dana Manciagli, author of *Cut the Crap, Get a Job!* and *Cut the Crap, Network for Success!* So first of all, thank you, Dana, for taking the time to speak with me and sharing some great advice about interview insights."

DM: "My pleasure. I'm looking forward to helping your readers as much as possible."

HG: "Thank you. So the first question I have is what would you like to share with people about steps to take to get a job, a job interview, or just an interview or appointment with a person who can help further them in their business or their career?"

DM: "Well, let's separate the two because they are slightly different. First of all, I'll share with you how to get a job interview, and then how to get an appointment with a networking contact. There are slight differences. To get a job interview, you need two things: I call them the front door and the backdoor execution. How you go through the front door to even get an interview is submitting a great application. Beyond a resume, this minimally consists of a unique cover letter. The cover letter should be less about you and all about them, the hiring company. You want to pivot your background on their job description. Now that's the front door, so you need to submit through the online website or LinkedIn or however they're asking to get into their system.

"The backdoor is critical. The backdoor is your networking to find connections. There're two really good things to look for and ask for with these connections. You need to find an employee at that company who will submit your same application through the employee referral system. So many jobs are secured that way. Alternatively, find a networking contact who will help get your

29

application directly to the hiring manager. LinkedIn, for example, is the best tool to do both of these. So you submit through the front door, meaning the way they want you to through HR or a recruiter, and then the backdoor is where you network or go through the employee referral system to get your credentials onto the desk of the decision maker.

"Now, you asked about how to get an appointment with a networking contact. You need to do a great request for a meeting. In a formal letter, please avoid writing things like 'Hi, I want to connect. Let's do coffee, let's do lunch.' All of that is way too informal, including the typical 'Can I come in and pick your brain?' We need to raise the bar and have a clear purpose and a short agenda for that 30 minute meeting that you're requesting. Ask them for only 30 minutes of their time, state what you would like to accomplish, list three topics you would like to discuss, and you'll have a higher likelihood of getting that meeting and way better results."

HG: "That was some really great advice. The second question I have for you is what secret steps should people do before their interview or appointment takes place?"

DM: "Excellent question. So I'll separate them again for interviews. There are no secrets, just pure hard work that most candidates don't do today at any age for any job. They're not being done, and they're very simple. All of you are going to say, 'Well, these are so basic.' Yes, they're basic. So why aren't you doing them?

"Number one, study – no, dissect – the job description, and prepare to discuss the skills and experiences you have that relate to their job description. So a step you do before the interview is spend time writing notes dissecting their job description so that you can talk about yourself in relation to them. Number two, study the company, their industry, and the division you're talking to. As an example, I worked in a division called OEM at Microsoft Original Equipment Manufacturers. Candidates would come into my office and ask what OEM stands for or what OEM does. All of that is readily available on the Internet and they lose points."

"So we've gone through number one, dissect the JD, job description. Number two, study their company, industry products, etc. Number three is prepare what you will wear well in advance. Try it on. Be sure it's pressed and that your shoes are shined, etc. Finally, number four, prepare what you will bring with you. You need a nice folio so you don't look disorganized. You should bring extra copies of your resume, a pad, and a pen because you will be taking notes. Have a briefcase and bottle of water. Have everything you need ready. To finish this question, for a network meeting, you need to prepare the agenda and no more than three good questions for a 30 minute meeting. There are your secrets. Research the people on LinkedIn and Twitter. And bring a pad and paper -- no technology -- for note taking. If you're not writing things down, then it must not be that important, and it's also discourteous."

HG: "I like that, and I'm sure it will help a lot of people reading this or listening. The third question I have is, what do you think is the most important thing people should do before a meeting with people of influence?"

DM: "It's going to be slightly repetitive, only I'll go into more detail. Often, walking into meetings that we all have in our companies, there's a printed agenda or something on the white board that says we're going to accomplish this, this, and this. You can come in with that. You would stand out and be different if you had an agenda. I'll give you three things to have on the agenda. Number one, share your purpose of the meeting with them. For example, 'I really need to learn about the aerospace industry, and I came to you because you're an expert.' Number two, give them an introduction to you. Be sure you're prepared to talk about yourself and describe your background in a concise manner. Not the hospital you were born in or your favorite sports and hobbies. You need to have a professional introduction, and ask them to introduce themselves. The third one is that you have thought through three great interesting questions to ask them, and take notes on all of the above."

HG: "That's great. I especially liked what you said about the white board. The fourth question I have is, what would you share with readers or listeners as inside tips before interviewing with Fortune 100 Companies?"

DM: "I love this one since I've been a hiring manager in Fortune 100's for decades. Here are my top three tips from the inside perspective. Number one, every move you make is a sample of how you would perform working for me or whoever you're interviewing with. I'm going to repeat that – every move you make is a sample. This ranges from the often poor grammar and typos on cover letters and e-mails to how you sound on the phone, if there's a dog barking in the background, how you shake hands, your posture, your answers, and much more.

"Number two, don't ever let your guard down or go off the record. So many candidates sabotage themselves by sharing too much information, making a bad joke, and sharing way more than what the interviewer asks. Our secret as an interviewer is to just stop talking and not stop them from talking. Some candidates will go on and on, and it just gets worse and worse. So one tip I'll share for a candidate is to say three important things, and then stop talking. Don't babble on and on.

"Finally, my third insider tip is to air on the formal side with all of your communication – your business attire, thank you notes, follow up, and everything in between. These are my insider tips."

HG: "Those were really good tips, and I liked the part of every move you make is a sample. The fifth question I have is, what is the most important thing interviewees should do after the meeting or interview?"

DM: "It's a real shame that so many candidates don't do anything for a variety of reasons. Some think they blew it and didn't get the job, so they don't bother writing a thank you note. That's really bad. You don't know that you blew it or if the company is late in writing some follow ups. Let's talk about the three steps. First, be sure you secure the contact information for the person you just met with. I hear so many of my clients say, 'Oh, I just left a great interview, but I didn't get his e-mail address.' It's your job to get that when you're in the meeting. Ask them for a card. Without that, it's going to be really hard to follow up. Number two is to send an e-mail thank you note within 24 hours. E-mail is not only acceptable, but it's preferred because you'll get that thank you note to them before they're huddling with all the interviewers to talk about all the candidates. Snail mail actually takes too long. Now in this e-mail thank you note, since you took notes during the interview, make the note personal by citing something they said. You see how important that pen and paper is? You just can't be effective as a candidate without really writing down everything. Don't forget in that thank you note to express your interest in the job.

"The third point is to follow up with that interviewer within three months, whether you got the job or not, or whether they were helpful or not. As a networker, you should add them to your network and not just disappear. Remember, all these people you're meeting in the interview process can become future helpful supporters of yours, so start building a network rhythm of communicating with them."

HG: "What can you share with us about your 'Career Mojo' that is in the National Business Journals?"

DM: "First, everybody should have a subscription to the National Business Journal to read about the companies and people on the move if you're in job search mode, want to get promoted, or are moving careers. This is the number one publication. It reaches over 11 million people and in 43 cities, so just go to bizjournal.com. I don't sell for them, and I don't make any money, so I know as much as it sounds like an advertisement, it is simply a recommendation to use this as a resource."

"Career Mojo is my nationally syndicated column in all 43 city business journals and our objective with this column is to provide practical 'how to' information about all things career related. So whether you're job searching, you're career changing, you have career challenges, you're moving a career forward, or you're a hiring manager, these articles and Q&A's are for you. I get to answer questions from readers and provide my expertise after 30 years of working in Fortune 100's and startups."

HG: "That's great, and that sounds like a really good publication that people can get some great advice from. The final question I have is, what tips would you like to share with readers and listeners to increase their chances at nailing that interview or meeting, and, as your book says, cutting the crap and getting a job? Where can they learn more?"

DM: "Well first, my website has a ton of helpful information including blogs, videos, a resource guide, and more, and that's simply my first name and last name, DanaManciagli.com. And then my book *Cut the Crap, Get a Job!* is on Amazon. It not only has an end-to-end job search process that I recommend from an inside perspective, but it comes with nine free template downloads that I designed for candidates to compete in today's tough market. So go grab the book, grab all the free information on DanaManciagli.com, and I believe that you will see greater success."

HG: "Thank you, Dana, for taking the time to share some really great advice that will help a lot of people."

DM: "My pleasure."

CHAPTER 8

THE MEETING
BEFORE THE MEETING

So you're finally meeting with the person who you feel can accelerate your career. It's taken weeks, and you may only have one opportunity to make that one great impression.

Most people only think of the person who they are meeting with. But there is something that I like to call the "meeting before the meeting," meaning that there are many others on the sidelines who may be influential in the decision to hire a potential employee.

Here are some tips for before you enter your actual meeting or interview:

1. Make sure you Google the person and the company you are meeting with. The more you know about them, the more you can converse about topics that will connect well with them. That's not to say, however, that you should be a stalker on their Facebook page.

2. Leave your house early, just in case of traffic delays, and get clear directions to your destination so that you can be there on time. I like to set my watch back by fifteen minutes to ensure promptness. I heard a line that rings true when it comes to meetings and interviews: "If you're early, you're on time. If you're on time, you're late."

3. After you arrive, the minute your car door shuts, consider yourself in the meeting. You don't know who just parked next to you, who is in the lobby with you, or who is riding the elevator with you on the way up. Have a smile on your face, and be polite to everyone.

4. Be especially nice to the receptionist and anyone else who may be working there. You may even want to get the receptionist's name and engage her in pleasant conversation. Of course, keep in mind that you do not want to come off as being insincere.

   My mom once relayed a technique that she used when conducting interviews for her business. She would have the interviewees sit in the lobby for about ten to fifteen minutes waiting for her to become available. She would pre-position a trusted staff member in the waiting room as well, to nonchalantly interact with them. In addition, the receptionist would purposely engage them in conversation while they waited. My mom wanted to know how they acted before they finally came through the door to see her with their "interview personalities" turned on, ready to win her over. She wanted to know how they acted when the spotlight wasn't on them.

5. Other reasons to be nice to the receptionist? If you call in at some point after the meeting, you may be more likely to have your call put through or be fit into the schedule for a future meeting if she remembers you as being a pleasant person.

6. Just like when you arrived at the office, when you leave the office, consider yourself still "on" until the car door closes and you drive away.

SO REMEMBER: Sometimes the person you are scheduled to meet with may not be the only important person you encounter that day. So at every interview or appointment, be just as nice to the people in the mailroom as the people in the boardroom because you never know who may have a vote.

CHAPTER 9

NETWORK, NETWORK, NETWORK

You know what they say - "It's not what you know, it's who you know."

When I am talking about networking, I am not talking about social networks, though social media can definitely be an asset. Right now, I am talking about good, old fashioned, face-to-face contact. There is nothing better than a good firm handshake and looking somebody in the eye.

When you sit at a desk all day long, you may not have the chance to expand your horizons in the work world. However when you are out and about, you often have the chance to connect with and learn from others that could lead to incredible opportunities. Make sure that you always carry business cards so that if you do connect with someone, you have an easy way of giving them your contact information. If you are young, you may want to use your parent's email address and telephone number for your safety. Ask for their card as well.

So what are the different ways that you can try to network?

One suggestion for getting out and meeting people is to pick up a social sport like golf or tennis. If you love basketball or hockey, you may want to check to see if there are adult sports leagues in your community. I personally enjoy the sport of golf and especially love taking part in golf tournaments. It is a great way to get out there for personal enjoyment and at the same time, network like crazy. Do you know how many business deals are done on the golf course each year?

If sports are not your thing, it can be something else that interests you, where you find a way to connect with others who have similar interests.

In addition to golf, I love music. When I first moved to Nashville, I didn't know a single person, so I joined the Nashville Youth Symphony and met over one hundred people my age with similar interests right off the bat. If you interact with people who have related interests, you will often form connections, which may lead to future opportunities.

People tend to trust and want to work with people they know and like. Again, sometimes it's not what you know, it can be who you know, or who your family knows, that may give you a leg up on the competition. If, for example, you have the exact same resume as another qualified candidate applying for a position, and the employer knows you personally or knows of you or your family, it may move you to the top of the list, putting you one step ahead of the game.

SO REMEMBER: Network, Network, Network!

Houston's Interview with Collin Brace

HG: "I am thrilled to be interviewing Collin Brace, Vice President of Sun Records, who will be sharing the importance of networking. Hey Collin, can you share with the readers and listeners tips on networking and how you network in your position as Vice President of Sun Records?"

CB: "Yes, I would be happy to. I think networking is so vital to today's business atmosphere and especially in my industry, the music industry, the entertainment industry. Networking is probably top tier, and one of the most important things you can focus on. The tips and the advice I would give would be:

"Be authentic. I think with where I am at, with the position I have at Sun Records, some people network just to network and some people are kind of viral networkers. It's all about 'Who can help me with what I am trying to do? . . . Who can get me the next phone number that I need? . . . Who will open their address book for me?' You know, I don't give a lot of respect to people who treat networking that way. If used in that way, it is kind of a 'used and be used' scenario. But the people who are genuine and want to start a relationship and want to get to know you on a level that is mutual, that kind of networking is very beneficial. It's especially helpful in an industry like entertainment or publishing where it really is important to know the people that you work with or the people who work for you and understanding who's on the other end of the telephone call. Those are very important things, especially as a leader. You need to know how to treat people and to know g more than just their value in connection with what they are working on, like the value they bring to the person or to the team.

"You also need to think about how can you be helpful to them? It is twofold. It is not always just what you can get out of someone, but also how can you be helpful to someone else? The best networking that I have ever seen is when I offer to be helpful to someone else. That may not be valuable to the project I am working on in the moment, but I do it just out of the genuineness of caring for the person. Peter Drucker is a big person that I take a lot of influence from, and he is known as the 'father of modern management.' One of the points that he really pushed in his later days was that management and marketing and networking are all about the people. Caring for the people on the other end of a project and not just viewing them as deadlines or obstacles, but as actual people. The people who approach networking like that will be very successful."

HG: "That is really excellent advice. Now my second question is, how has networking changed your life?"

CB: "It has been extremely important to my success. I would be the first one to say that 99% of my success in life is due to other people helping me and other people being very kind in opening their rolodex or staying an extra hour at the end of the day or offering to help on a project and offering advice or coming along side me and helping me choose the right direction vs. the wrong direction or giving me a little bit of insight because they have been there before. Networking in that respect has single handedly changed whether I was successful at something or whether I was going to fail. At the end of the day, it is really about the people who have come alongside me and invested in me as a person that I owe all the gratitude to. It has been something that I really appreciate at the end of the day, all the people that have invested in me. They had no reason to. It was just out of the goodness of their heart and the character of their upbringing and their business morals. Those are the people that are the winners for me."

HG: "What would you recommend to readers and listeners as the first steps to start networking in their business or position?"

CB: "My recommendation would be: Half of life is just showing up, and the other half is listening and being prepared. A lot of networking happens when you 'SHOW UP.' When you commit to going to that party that you did not want to go to, or going to that event that you are not sure is beneficial. Going with an open mind is important, as is not only thinking of what you can get out of it, but what you can give of yourself for the betterment of your industry. Those people will make really good strides in their industry and in their profession. Even in school, the first step is to show up.

"The second step is to 'FOLLOW UP.' When someone says 'Call' or 'I am available,' or 'Do you want to go to lunch, hit me up,' DO IT. So many people have said to me, 'Sure let's go to lunch sometime - here is my e-mail or just give me a call,' I take them up on it because that is their invitation to getting to know me and me getting to know them. It surprises me when I hear that people don't follow up. A buddy of mine said one time, 'Yeah, he gave me his card, and he said e-mail him.' I asked, "Well, did you email him?' and he said, 'No, I haven't gotten around to it.' That is crazy. You never know what will come of that relationship if you are genuine and authentic about it. It is an unbelievable fact that people just don't follow up. So first, SHOW UP. Second, FOLLOW UP. Those would be my two pieces of advice for beginners in networking."

HG: "That is great advice! I am so thankful that I met you at a music conference in Nashville last year, and we were able to stay in touch through networking and business lunches and appointments. You had offered to mentor me and I was, and am, very grateful and honored. The fourth question I have for you is, what would you suggest others do if they are looking to network and find a mentor?"

CB: "I think that finding a mentor is difficult. I have two very important mentors in my life, and it took a very intentional mindset in me to look, to find, and to seek out the mentors that came along side me, passed along wisdom, and were there as a sounding board in times of difficulty and times of success. My suggestion if someone is looking for a mentor is, anytime someone says give me a call or says let's meet up, follow through with that. Typically, we don't know where our mentors are going to come from.

"The other part of that is, if you find someone like a professor or older person in your life that you really respect and you feel you could really learn from and they have wisdom to give to you, don't be afraid to ask. A lot of times, those people are never asked. They are never approached or asked to take 10 minutes to sit down and give their top three pieces of advice in this business or in this industry or in life.

"Both of the mentors I have are extremely successful guys in business, but they align with me in my faith, in my family life, my spirituality, my morals, my ethics, and my values as a person. That is very important, because a lot of times in life when you hit that road block or challenge and you wish you had an older person to give you wisdom, it is really great to know that they align with your values and see the ins and outs of your business.

"On that topic, it does not have to be someone directly in your industry. One of the mentors I go to is in publishing, one is in consulting, and I am in the music industry. It is actually very helpful because the advice they offer is very broad and global, and it's up to me to specifically apply it to my industry. Don't be afraid to ask someone. Seek out those people.

"Another thing is that a mentor could be someone that is no longer living. I have a lot of mentors who had written books hundreds of years ago. They are not even alive, and they are still mentoring me in my mind, my heart, and my soul, and I think that is important because we can get caught up in 'I want this face-to-face or one-on-one time.' For some people, it is difficult to do that because of scheduling or time of life or the season. Sometimes it is just good enough to find a mentor in a podcast or someone you follow on YouTube. I have those kinds of mentors as well. Those are great places to start.

"The last point to make about finding a mentor is also to realize you are always in a spot to be a mentor, and if you are unwilling to give back to someone younger than you or someone just getting started with something you have a lot of experience in, then don't expect someone else to give you their time. It's a two way street. To be mentored you must mentor others, and it's a constant mentor/mentoree code that is always going on. You have to always find those people to give back to, and find the time for the people who want to gain from you. Even if you are a teenager, there are always younger kids who look up to you and see you as an example, and they are always on the mark for that. So, again, don't be afraid to ask. Look for mentors in other things than just the physical person. Be a mentor. Those would be my three things."

HG: "Thank you for that insight! Now for my fifth question, what other information would you like to share about networking with the listeners and readers, especially those who may want to get into the music or entertainment industry?"

CB: "Find out where others in your industry go to do business or network. If it is conferences that happen in your industry around your area, then go to those conferences. In the entertainment industry, a lot of networking happens in the studio or at a show or sometimes it can happen at a conference or a summit that might be around your area. I guess the biggest piece of advice for the music or entertainment industry is that there are the non-traditional networking things that are out there like Facebook and YouTube and LinkedIn if you are on the professional side of the industry. Those are resources that are freely available. A lot of times, people do not take advantage of them to the fullest, but there are people who do really get the most out of what is available.

"Houston, you and I met because of an Americana Fest. I happened to be on a panel. You happened to be there because of an artist we were representing. You came up to me afterwards, and you told me who you were. It was very obvious that you were on to something – you were going somewhere – and I wanted to learn more of what you were doing and going through. Just having the courage of showing up, following through, and asking, those are the tips that can really make the difference in effectively utilizing the people who are in your industry.

"I think those are the best scenarios. Show up, go to that show that you do not really know if you want to go to. Stay after the show and talk to the band. All the bands in the world love talking to the fans from Coldplay down to the local artist at your pub. They all love to talk to people after the show. Try to talk to those people. Tell them what you are up to. Tell them what you are doing. Ask them questions. Find those circles of other people that are doing things you are interested in doing. Start getting into those circles. Push your way through, ask to be involved, ask to be a part of it. Be brave and courageous. Half of the time it is just, again, showing up and asking."

HG: "Sun Records holds the library for some pretty big names and their music, such as Johnny Cash, Elvis, Jerry Lee Lewis, and more. How do you and your company network?"

CB: "Very much the same as above. I am going to go back to 'Be authentic.' I think that with the brands that my record label represents (Johnny Cash, Elvis Presley, and Jerry Lee Lewis) you HAVE to be authentic to those brands and be genuine to their listeners and the audiences that those artists have. It may require you to move outside your comfort zone. For me, I grew up always listening to Johnny Cash, so it is really easy for me to relate to the Johnny Cash world and the Rockabilly world. But I did not grow up listening to Elvis, so it was uncomfortable for me to try to connect with and understand the Elvis audience.

"What I had to do was jump in with both feet and really be unafraid of listening to something or doing something that I may not like or to try to connect with people that I may not really understand. But what happens with that is you grow, and I started to have this love for Elvis – for what he did in the industry, for his story and how he came about. If you do not have a love for learning, then it is going to be very difficult for you to connect with things that you may be required to connect to in your industry.

"As for the company, the company does a lot of things. My boss or I will go to a conference and before the conference, a big part of networking is researching who is going to be there. That may require e-mailing a person you may be working on a project with and saying, 'Hey are you going to be going to this conference? I know we have not ever met but can we meet up here? Let's get a time on the books.' You've got to really meet up with that person in person.

"Another example is that I do a lot of licensing. There is a big licensing conference in Vegas every year, and what we try to do is whoever is going to the conference beforehand we go through our rolodex and look at all the people that we are doing licensing deals with that have representation at that conference. Then we send them all an invitation to meet up. It may be a ten minute meeting, it may just be a cup of coffee or a beer afterwards, but we really intentionally make a commitment to see those people and ask what their needs are. Next, we assess where we might fit into their projects or their campaigns for the year, and then let them know what our needs are and let them know where we are at. Then, it is really easy to meet up with somebody because we have got some things to talk about. Those are the ways that you network within a company. I would say it is similar in most other industries."

HG: "That is some excellent advice and my final question for you is, is there anything else you would like to share with the readers and listeners, and where can they go learn more?"

CB: "You know, right now I am really hyped up on this book by Bob Buford, who wrote the book *Halftime*. He also wrote a new book called *Drucker and Me*. Bob is a man that I have not met yet, but he has been a mentor to one of my mentors, and so I got an early read on the book and part of the book is a story about how Bob Buford was mentored by Peter Drucker, who I mentioned earlier. He has the Peter Drucker Institute and has been a consultant for loads of companies from General Motors to General Electric. He is just an unbelievable professor and writer, and Bob Buford tells the story of when he met Peter Drucker and all the advice and really cool facts in connection with being mentored by him. So it is very appropriate to mention this book because it is very much about networking and the mentor/mentee relationship. Also look up anything by Peter Drucker, he has a ton of books. Some I haven't read yet, but some I have, and they have been very valuable resources. Those are the two resources I am really hot on right now, and the two guys I would look up."

HG: "Excellent, thank you again, Collin, for taking time out of your day to share with the readers and listeners advice about networking."

CB: "You bet, I am very excited for what is to come, and I cannot wait to read this new book, Houston, when it comes out, and let me know if there is anything I can do to help you."

HG: "Will do, thank you so much."

CHAPTER 10

FOLLOW UP

Following up can be extremely important after you establish a connection with someone.

Most of us come into contact with many new people each week, and while you may remember some of the people that you have come into contact with, they may or may not remember you. If you want to stand out to a particular person that you encountered, then you need to go the extra mile to follow up, ensuring that you are memorable to them.

Obviously, if a person you have connected with does not remember you down the road, your efforts and time (and remember, time is money) will have gone to waste.

First, send them a friendly e-mail saying how nice it was to meet them.

Next, check to see if they are on social media. "Like" their company page on Facebook or send them a friend request if you feel it would be appropriate. You may want to follow the person on Twitter as well, and interact with them on occasion there.

Then see if they are on LinkedIn and, again, if appropriate, connect with them there.

On LinkedIn, you can join groups, and often others who know you or have worked with you in the past will endorse you for certain skills. If you are looking to be hired and your potential employer is someone who trusts LinkedIn, this can only help.

I also believe in the good, old-fashioned hand written thank you note. That can go a long way to show that you are a person with manners, and you will stand out, since not many people take the time to write personal notes. When the person you are following up with is older, this is definitely a nice touch since this is the etiquette that they were likely brought up with.

If you feel that it is appropriate, another great way to follow up would be to invite the person to lunch or coffee. That additional personal interaction will give you the chance to speak one on one, and you will have that person's undivided attention for a period of time, which could ultimately result in a home run. Choose a place that you can afford, since it's always a nice touch if you can pick up the tab. In addition, make sure that the place you choose is very convenient for the other person. If they have to drive across town, they may not wish to take the time. If they can walk across the street from their office, they are more inclined to say yes to your invitation.

SO REMEMBER: Always follow up so that you're not just a faded memory, you're memorable.

Houston's Interview with Kaitlin Lindsey

HG: "I have Kaitlin Lindsey, Executive Vice President for PR with Icon Builder Media, who will be sharing some tips on the importance of following up. As a publicist, Kaitlin has represented Alan Alda, the Trans-Siberian Orchestra, TNT and TBS, and AMC Networks. Kaitlin, first of all, thank you for sharing time to give us your professional tips and insight on following up in the business world. What would you like to share with the readers and listeners about what you feel is the most important thing about following up in your world?"

KL: "Well my pleasure, Houston, and I am so happy to have a chance to speak with you. The most important thing in terms of following up is really about building relationships, because ultimately who you're following up with are people you're going to want to know in the future. You want to be referred by these people to other people as well. I always like to say that there is a thin line between stalking and restraining orders. You want to be aggressive to a certain extent, but you also have to know when to back off."

HG: "Very true, very true. My second question for you is, if you could describe yourself in three words, what would those words be?"

KL: "I would say I am very driven, I'm honest, and very compassionate. I think that helps in my profession with follow up because you have to be driven to want to really get to the right person, and you don't just want to take no for an answer. You also have to be honest with the people you are speaking to and what you are following up on and be able to have them trust you. Like a car salesman, a lot of people don't trust publicists because they might think they may be dishonest; there is that stereotype. You want to come off as your true self, be sincere, and then people will trust the information you are trying to get to them and be more open with you. I think that is really important. Also be compassionate, because you want to understand the people that you are trying to get in touch with. Understand their time and where they're coming from, and be able to relate to them because they are going to be more apt to open up to you then as well."

HG: "Are there steps that the average person can take to improve their 'Follow Up' skills?"

KL: "I think this is a follow up from the last question, in a sense. You need to really value peoples' time. It is important to be very concise and to the point. Also, you need to know what you are asking and also the response that you're looking for, which isn't always necessarily the response you want. You need to understand that when you get on that follow up call, that you have enough information to move forward to the next step. You have to really know what you're asking for, and then again know the response that will help things move along."

HG: "How organized do you need to be to have a great 'Follow Up'?"

KL: "This is very important. You have to be extremely organized. A lot of it, again, is about building relationships, so if you are calling someone for follow up and then you are not organized, you're going to lose credibility. You want to demonstrate by example that you know what you are talking about, that there is a method to the madness, and that, again, you understand peoples' time. Also, with follow up, you want to be able to know exactly where it was you left off with that person. For me working in Public Relations, I am constantly talking to reporters and pitching various stories, but there are certain reporters that I am pitching three different stories to, so I have to know what the last story I was speaking about to this reporter was. I have to know what their last response was. If they said they were not interested, and I call back and I am pitching them the same story, I am going to lose creditability, and I am going to lose that relationship which ultimately will hurt the client. So you just want to be very on point!"

HG: "I completely get it. My fifth question for you is, is there anything else you would suggest to the readers and listeners as a must have for 'Follow Up' skills?"

KL: "I think it is really important to be conversational and to engage with the other person on the phone. Even if it is on the phone or via e-mail, again building relationships. You don't want to come off as a robot. People like talking to people. They don't like having these automated answering machines and such. So speak, obviously, in a very professional way, know what you are talking about, but engage. You want to create a conversation so that ultimately you are creating that bond with the other person. And then in the future, when you follow up with them again you can relate back to that conversation you had earlier on. And, even though it may be outside of business, know where the person is from, or just be able to recall earlier conversations, and show you actually care about the person and that you're listening to what they have to say."

HG: "That's excellent - and now my final question for you Kaitlin. What is the one BIG secret you can share for a successful 'Follow Up' that everybody needs to do starting today?"

KL: "You have to know your facts. You have to know what you are talking about. You also have to anticipate what the follow up questions will be from the person on the other side because they're, in turn, going to ask you questions that you need to be prepared for and be able to reply to without hesitation. You have to constantly think ahead two or three steps, and anticipate what they could possibly ask you. Then by having a quick, knowledgeable, thoughtful reply that establishes creditability and that establishes that the person you are following up with is the right person to follow up with, you'll be leaps and bounds ahead."

HG: "Thank you again, Kaitlin, for sharing your follow up advice with the readers and listeners."

KL: "You're welcome, Houston. My pleasure."

CHAPTER 11

THE PHONE

The telephone. It sounds simple, but there is a lot to think about.

There are four things I want to address:

1. Leaving a message for a potential employer or business contact;
2. Having a professional voicemail greeting for your callers;
3. Conducting business over the phone; and
4. Being interviewed over the phone.

1. Let's first talk about leaving a message for a potential employer or business contact on their voice mail. You should always leave your full name. Even if you think they know you, you may not be the only Steve they know. Next, don't ramble. Know what you want to say and get it out – short and to the point. And don't forget to leave your call back number, and then repeat it once again to give them time to grab a pen, or to double check the digits they wrote down the first time you said it.

2. As for your voicemail, make sure you sound professional with your personal greeting and don't have noise or music in the background when you are recording. In addition, for the most professional, polished image possible, keep your voicemail message as short as possible, and don't have a song playing before your greeting begins. People just might hang up because nobody likes wasting time.

3. As far as conducting business over the phone, I have several tips. First, make sure to call on a land line whenever possible. It is annoying to the other caller when cell phones cut out and it is almost always embarrassing to have to call back. Second, make sure you are in a quiet place. If you are calling from home, make sure your household is on mute. In others words, don't have your television on or people talking in the background. I always make sure, for example, that my dog is somewhere where he won't bark in the middle of the call.

If you need to speak with several people at once, there is free conference call-in numbers that you can use in order to facilitate your call.

4. Sometimes you may need to do interviews over the phone. This could be anything from a job interview, or, recently, I have been doing phone interviews to promote my book. Again, whenever possible, make sure to call on a landline from a quiet environment. Second, if you are being interviewed, the interviewer does not have the luxury of seeing you in person and you don't have the luxury of using your winning smile or looking them in the eye. The way you come across in what you say and the tone of your voice will mean everything. So speak intelligently, don't ramble on, stay on topic, and I recommend standing up to keep your voice energized.

SO REMEMBER: The phone may seem like a simple, every day thing, but if used correctly, it can be a very important part of the way you conduct business.

CHAPTER 12

DRESS FOR SUCCESS

I'm sure many of you out there have heard the expression "Dress for success." What does that exactly mean? Does that mean always dressing in a suit and tie if you are male or wearing a nice dress or a business suit if you are female?

There was a time not long ago when suit and tie was the norm for almost every occasion. When men and women boarded a flight, they were dressed in their Sunday best. And look at footage of old baseball games. The men were dressed like they walked off Wall Street.

But over time, the concept of dressing for success has changed. Does that mean you no longer have to dress up? The answer depends on your occupation, what you are doing, and the impression you are trying to make at that moment.

A professional athlete will go to work in the uniform with which he was provided. A lifeguard would look ridiculous sitting atop his lifeguard chair wearing anything other than a bathing suit. These are obvious examples, just like a fireman, military personnel, or other jobs where a certain type of uniform or clothing are required.

In the business world, however, there are often certain standards. Let's discuss how to put your best foot forward and always dress for success. There is a fine line between being overdressed and being underdressed. You have to find the happy medium, considering what is age and gender appropriate.

When you are meeting someone for the first time professionally or going on an interview, you may want to dress in business attire, taking into account where and who you are meeting.

If you are the front person for your own company or you are a "personality," you may want to brand your image.

If you are working at a company on a daily basis, you will want to adhere to the tone of the company and dress appropriately. Take your cues from your superiors. At many businesses, the norm is "business casual" which essentially means dressing neatly and nicely without overdoing it. And, it is often believed that if you dress up a bit, you will feel better about yourself, rise to a higher standard of professionalism, and be on your "A" game. So as long as you are not truly overdressing, there is nothing wrong with looking nice.

There are certain parts of the country where the standards for business attire differ. In Manhattan, for example, people tend to dress sharply in the business world. In Los Angeles, on the other hand, people often go to work in much more casual attire. In Honolulu, formal business wear includes a flower "Aloha" shirt.

For me, when I go to a business meeting, I tend to wear what I consider "business casual" attire – Typically nice slacks, a polo shirt and dress shoes, as opposed to tennis shoes. When I go to a book signing or a press interview, however, I often wear the same shirt that is the front cover of the book I am speaking about. For my first book, my shirt was a blue and white plaid shirt. I made that look part of my marketing and branding. I am not in my basketball shorts and I am not in my tennis shoes. I am also not dressed in a suit and tie. I am dressed age appropriately, and during a book signing, I can be easily spotted and recognized because of the shirt. If you saw me at school or at a bookstore shopping on any other day, I would likely be dressed like any other average teen.

SO REMEMBER: In order to dress for success, observe those in your industry. Don't under or overdo, and be age appropriate.

CHAPTER 13

THE INTERNET: FRIEND OR FOE?

In today's world, most people, especially young people, spend a considerable amount of time on the Internet for everything from research to e-mail and social networking.

First and foremost, once something is on the Internet, it is permanent. There are no take backs. So be very sure that you never put anything out there that could ever come back to haunt you. As I like to say, "That picture you take or the post you make just could be a viral mistake!"

Do you know that many employers (including potential employers) and colleges check social media to get a glimpse of who you really are? If there is something you are about to post that you would not want a potential employer or college admissions officer to see, you'd better think twice.

This can also be said for potential business partners. They may judge you by what you have posted on social media.

If you are a businessperson, keep your personal life off your business page, and if a friend posts something inappropriate, delete the post.

And use common sense! Don't let the world know when you are going out of town and your house is empty because you never know who may be scouring social network sites for easy homes to break into.

Now, how can you use the Internet as your friend?

For one thing, you can find leads from the Internet to build your business.

You can also use the Internet and social media sites for marketing purposes. For example, ads can be posted on sites like Facebook and targeted to a specific demographic. And one of the easiest ways to market to potential customers is by using Twitter. And the best part of Twitter? It's free!

You can also establish a company website to build a fan base and even use that website to sell product or have it linked to other websites with similar, but non-competing, interests.

SO REMEMBER: The Internet can be an amazing tool to help you build your business, but be very careful because what you put out there may stay out there forever.

Houston's Interview with Marc Guberti

HG: "I have a special guest, Marc Guberti, also a 16 year old entrepreneur and author. Marc, can you share some of your success in connection with the Internet and social media?"

MG: "I have a thriving blog about business and social media that gets close to one thousand visitors every day. Most of my blog's traffic comes from my social networks such as Twitter and Pinterest, where I have thousands of followers, and they're growing at a rapid pace. So that is my success on the Internet -- a blog which promotes some of the books I've written, and my social networks which build traffic to my blog."

HG: "That's great, and congratulations on all that success."

MG: "Thank you."

HG: "How do you think people can make the Internet their friend?"

MG: "Well, the best way to make the Internet your friend is by utilizing features, such as social networks, that you would not have without the Internet. It is important to use the features that are exclusive and only able to be found on the Internet, and do your best to make the world a better place."

HG: "That is amazing advice. My third question for you is, how can people prevent the Internet from becoming their foe?"

MG: "Well, this is a really good question. In order to prevent the Internet from becoming your foe, you need to specialize at certain things on the Internet. A common mistake is to create an account on every single social network. That means you have to go to different social networks to make different connections, and you have to learn different things about each social network. I believe that it is better to have one hundred followers on a single social network, than ten followers on ten different social networks. So, specialize in what you do instead of just trying to create an account on every single social network and trying to be everything to everyone."

HG: "One of your books is titled *How to be Successful on Twitter*. Can you share one or two of the top things that people can do to be successful on Twitter?"

MG: "The two best ways to become successful on Twitter are, first, to get a targeted following, and, second, engage with those followers.

"There are three kinds of followers on Twitter, but most people only know two of them -- the fake follower and the real follower. The fake follower is just a number that people use to make themselves look bigger than they really are. The real follower is also a number, but someone you can engage with.

"The third kind of follower, which most people don't think about, is the targeted follower. The targeted follower is the best follower of them all because the targeted follower is someone that shares your same industry or occupation and is generally interested in what you were tweeting about before following you. For me, my targeted followers are people who are interested in social media, business, and blogging. This results in them taking a stronger interest in my tweets.

"In order to engage with your followers, be sure to build a targeted following because that helps out a lot with the engagement. This can especially be helpful when people mention you on Twitter, whether they share one of your articles or whether they just want to say 'hi' or 'thanks for the follow.' Respond to those people because you never know how long a conversation is going to last on Twitter. To get targeted followers, find someone in your niche with over 100,000 followers, and follow that person's followers who are likely to follow back and engage with your followers by asking questions, having pictures in your tweets, and consistently tweeting."

HG: "Acquiring targeted followers is definitely important! Since we are both 16 years old right now, with the advancements in technology, where do you see the Internet and social media 16 years from now?"

MG: "It's hard to imagine where the Internet and technology are going to be 16 years from now, but I'm going to give my opinion as to where I see it. Right now, few teenagers are aware of the potential of building businesses and creating products on the Internet. Some of them believe that the whole process is getting a job after college and going from there. The problem with that is that there are no set goals and no vision. I predict that in these 16 years, more teenagers will be on the Internet and creating businesses because the awareness of the fact that you can be successful as a teenager. Even in middle school, high school, or college, it is very possible to be successful and social media will be a big factor in that. It will turn from, in my opinion, a tool of socializing into a tool for people to reach out to entrepreneurs and make connections.

"A problem is that social media is slowly going into an automated phase where people are scheduling tweets in bulk. What people need to do is tweet at the moment, as well as scheduling tweets. There are more people who are sending automated tweets and not sending tweets at the moment, allowing them to engage in conversations with their followers. Sixteen years from now social media, in my prediction, is not going to be as social, but staying social on social media is the key to success on any network."

HG: "Marc, are there any last secrets to social media success you would like to share?"

MG: "There are two things I would like to say. The first thing is that we all have the dream, the illusion, or anything you would like to call it, where we see ourselves with the big blue verified check mark. We would love 100,000 followers, while only following 100 people because you see all the celebrities do it so you think why not me? The problem is that many people do not know about you yet on social media, which is why it is important to follow people. I remember being stuck at -- I remember the exact number actually -- 1,667 followers for many months. Then I started to follow people, and I got more followers as well.

"Another thing to remember about social networks is that you need to be persistent in order to experience success. You are not going to go from zero followers today to getting 100,000 followers the next day. For most people, it takes years to get 100,000 followers. So you need to be persistent. Engage with your followers every day, follow targeted users, and you will eventually see the numbers that you have always dreamed of on your social networks."

HG: "That is some great advice and something that I have even learned with my journey. Now my final question for you - if people would like to learn more, where can they contact you?"

MG: "I will be available at any time to discuss business, social media, and blogging on my Twitter handle @MarcGuberti. You can also contact me at my blog at www.Marcguberti.com where I publish two blog posts every day at 9am and 9pm Eastern. I also have several books on Amazon including *How to be Successful on Twitter*, which was previously discussed. I have other books about business and social media as well."

HG: "That's great, and thank you Marc for the interview and sharing your tips on shooting for success to all the readers and listeners."

MG: "Thank you for having me for the interview Houston."

CHAPTER 14

A DOZEN TIPS FOR WORKPLACE CONDUCT

Getting along with others in the workplace is crucial. You want to be a pleasant person to be around, and I believe that the following tips are important:

1. Be respectful of other people's time in the office. Don't be a nuisance. For example, if you have questions for your boss, don't go into her office every ten minutes asking questions. Collect everything you want to speak to her about and do it all at one time during the day. Further, don't be that person in the office that stands at people's desks just to shoot the breeze. I call them the "Time Takers." Most people feel badly asking the Time Taker to leave but, it is annoying having a Time Taker taking up your valuable work time. The longer they hang out, often the more annoying and uncomfortable it becomes, until people start to avoid the Time Taker. If <u>you</u> have a Time Taker taking up your time, do not hesitate to politely tell them to take a time out.

2. Be confident but not cocky. There is nothing worse than a person who always feels that they know better in every situation. No one likes a know it all.

3. Take the time to listen to the opinions of others because you just may learn something and you just might grab a golden nugget that you could use someday.

4. Do not take credit for something that somebody else has done – that's just not cool.

5. Be organized. Always. Good organizational skills will go a long way in making sure you get the job done and that you do not fall behind. Use a calendar and reminders to make sure you never miss deadlines.

6. Realize that your superiors are people that you should respect, but not necessarily be intimidated by. I used to be scared of my teachers, for example, and then, after getting to know one of my teachers outside of school, I realized that instead of being the "almighty teacher," she was a person, like I am a person, with a mom, dad, sister, brother and a life.

7. Own up to your mistakes. Everyone makes mistakes. Don't try to blame your mistake on someone else. Many people refuse to take personal accountability for their actions, and that is wrong. Own up to it, apologize if need be, and learn from it.

8. Be tolerant of other races, religions and political ideas. Even if you have a different personal opinion than some of your colleagues, don't put others down and don't shove your beliefs down other people's throats. Never make racist jokes or say anything that could be seen as offensive, even if you didn't mean it that way. As your mother likely told you, "If you don't have anything nice to say, don't say anything at all."

9. Stay in the loop, but avoid gossip. You can be sure that anything you say in a gossipy manner will get back to the person that is being spoken about. Not only will they not appreciate it, but often times, what goes around, comes around. And if you go around spreading information that was

told to you in confidence, it more than likely will end up that you will be known as a person that cannot be trusted.

10. If you go on a business lunch with colleagues, do not order alcohol or, if you are encouraged by your colleagues to order alcohol, do not drink to the point where you become inebriated.

11. When eating at a restaurant, be sure to never act rude or condescending to the waiter or waitress. People often judge others by how they treat people serving them.

12. Likewise, do not act in a condescending or rude manner to people that are in positions lower than you at the company. The person in the mailroom just may be your colleague one day.

SO REMEMBER: Be considerate and respectful of everyone so that you are respected in return.

CHAPTER 15

LISTEN UP!

Today I want to talk to you about the lost the art of listening. Are you hearing that?!

One of the most important skills in business, and maybe even in life, is being a good listener. The best communicators are said to be those who listen versus those who talk too much.

Listening is an active process. It doesn't mean quietly sitting and staring at the person across from you. You need to say and do things to let them know that you are truly "hearing" what they have to say. It can be a simple nod of your head, or simply saying "I understand" or "Go on…" Be present. Don't daydream. Really make a conscious effort to hear what they are saying.

I always try to be a sponge and absorb as much as I can from the people who know more than I do.

If you have a boss, you want to hear their expectations of you in general, and on particular projects. If you have employees, you want to hear their questions, requests and even complaints, to maintain a healthy, positive work environment. If you have customers, listen very attentively to their wants and needs - because to maintain those customers, they often need to feel like "the customer is always right."

Sometimes people are not clear on what they are trying to say to you, so being a good listener also means that at times, you need to read between the lines and pick up body language cues in order to understand what they are really telling you.

SO REMEMBER: Always listen up!

Houston's Interview with Annetta Wilson

HG: "I have a special guest, Annetta Wilson, President of Annetta Wilson Media Training & Success Coaching, who will be sharing some tips on successful communication. Annetta, thanks for being here. You have been in the communications world your entire career. How important is the art of listening to you?"

AW: "Well it's my pleasure Houston, and thank you so much for including me. There are two parts to communication. There's what you say, and then there's how it's received. Often, the confusion comes when what you say isn't received the way you mean it. So being an active listener is just as important as being a communicator."

HG: "What is the most important thing you've learned and want to share about how to be successful in business by listening to others?"

AW: "Well, I can tell you the way it works for my business. I let my clients tell me what they need by asking questions and listening, and then I create the program and services that fit their needs. Otherwise, I would just be guessing. I always go through the process of asking people where they are stuck, what their problem areas are, what they would like to improve upon, and then I look for themes. When I keep hearing the same thing over and over again, that's when I know that I need to create a product, training, or coaching program that addresses those needs. So I listen first, then I create."

HG: "That's great. Besides listening, what are other communication skills people should know and do well in order to reach their desired level of success?"

AW: "Research who you are talking to. What are their interests? In what industry do they work? What things are they passionate about? What groups or organizations do they belong to? Where did they go to school? Those kinds of things are called psychographics, not just demographics. The demographics are age, race, religion, and those sorts of things. But you want to try to figure out what their life is about. What do they orient their life around? That will tell you the kinds of things that are important to them and give you some great places to begin conversations. Everyone's favorite topic is themselves. When you get people talking about themselves, they will tell you just about anything and everything you need to know. So be more interested *in* people than trying to be interesting *to* them."

HG: "When you are interviewing people for media or press interviews, what do you feel is the most important asset to share with them as well as the viewers?"

AW: "Their passion about their topic. You can be the best at whatever you do, but if you deliver it in a dry, boring way people are not going to feel you. When I say 'feel you,' I'm talking about non-verbal communication. According to the research done by Dr. Albert Mehrabian, over half of our communication is non-verbal. It's what we normally call body language. So if you're not enthusiastic, if you're not emotionally invested in what you're talking about, no one else will be either. So be excited about the gifts, skills, and abilities you've been given, and people will just follow you anywhere."

HG: "That's great information. My next question today is, as a trainer and speaker, do you feel it is very important to be aware of the audience's attention and to keep them tuned in and listening?"

AW: "I can't train without tuning in to the audience. I walk in knowing what I want to teach, but I always ask first what it is about this topic the audience really wants to know. I write those things down even if I planned a curriculum. There are some things I'm going to teach anyway depending on the subject matter, but what they tell me in that room determines the direction we go in. If what I'm teaching isn't relevant, they're going to check out. So I always include my audience in what I'm doing. You shouldn't be teaching anything that you're not good at or not really familiar with. Otherwise that's a very scary prospect. Always keep checking in to see if they're learning, see if they have questions, and don't be afraid if they do have a question. That just shows they want to know more."

HG: "Can you share with the readers or listeners your secret sauce to being a master at communicating?"

AW: "I take my cues from people. I'm looking, I'm listening, I'm watching, I'm paying attention to body language cues and facial expressions, and I like to let people lead. In other words, if we're talking about a topic and they say something that really gets them excited, I'm going to ask them more questions about that. I have found, not only in my career as a journalist, but in my business in helping people learn to communicate more powerfully, that you should listen twice as much as you talk. You have two ears and one mouth, and you should use them accordingly."

HG: "That is some really excellent advice. The final question I have for you - Where can people contact you if they want to learn more about being a better communicator?"

AW: "Well thank you for asking Houston. My website is Speakwithease.com, and they can always call my office at 407-710-8989 if they have any questions about my coaching or training programs. If they go to my website, there is a free gift waiting for them. So I hope they're intrigued enough to find out what it is, so Speakwithease.com."

HG: "Excellent, and thank you again, Annetta, for taking your time to share all this excellent advice with the readers and listeners."

AW: "Thank you for inviting me to be a part of this project, Houston."

CHAPTER 16

WHEN YOU WORK FOR YOURSELF, YOU MAKE YOURSELF RICH

Today I want to talk to you about my Grandma Linda's favorite quote and what she has told me since I was very little - "When you work for others you make them rich, when you work for yourself you make yourself rich!"

When I was in Kindergarten my teacher told the whole class to go home and see if our grandparents would ask their bosses for the day off to come to our school lunch for Grandparents' Day.

I could not wait to get home that day and ask my Grandma Linda. I raced to her house right after school and asked her, just as I was told to do by my teacher. But her reply had me confused. I remember this being such a big "ah-ha" moment in my life.

My Grandma Linda saw this opportunity as a learning experience for me. Little did she know how big of an impact it would have! She turned the tables on me and asked, "Where do you think I work, and who do you think I am I supposed to ask?"

I did not have an answer for her -- I was just doing what my teacher had told me to do and asked her again to ask her boss for the day off so that she could come to Grandparents' Day. My grandma would not let up. She asked me again - "Who am I asking, and Houston, where do I work?"

She had a nice house, nice car and gave me nice Christmas and birthday presents so I figured that she had to work somewhere. But it then occurred to me that I did not know where she worked or even what she did exactly!

This is where Grandma Linda took the opportunity to the next level and said "Houston, I work every day, however I don't go to 'work', and I don't have to ask anyone for the day off or answer to them." By the puzzled look on my face, she knew that I clearly did not understand how this could be.

She then walked with me to her kitchen table, pointed to a pile of files, papers, and her phone, and told me that this is where she worked. She said she works hard every day, but is her own boss and does her own projects as a developer in the commercial real estate world.

She explained to me that she makes her own appointments and meetings, does her own schedule and can take the day off for Grandparents' Day without having to ask anyone for the day off.

Phew – At the time, I was mainly relieved that my grandma could come to my school lunch for Grandparents' Day.

I then asked my grandma what she was currently working on and she said, "I'll show you." I just thought she was going to show me a picture or some of her paperwork but instead she said, "Hop in the car, and let's go see a few of the projects I am working on." She then drove me to some buildings in our city and started telling me the story of how they got there or whom she sold them to or how she built them.

My grandma then asked me if I knew the building where my new doctor's office was and I replied that I did. She said that she worked on that property so that the medical building could actually be built there.

She then asked if I remembered the highway road construction and all of the workers that had been working on the intersection over the past few months. When I replied "yes," she told me that it was her project as well, and that she hired those workers to do all the work on the intersection to get the project done.

I said "Really?!" She must have thought I did not believe her! She then asked me if I had ever seen her name inside the main doorway of the building on a plaque as a thank you for a large donation she made to the hospital to make that deal happen, so that our town could get its first large medical building with doctors' offices in it.

We then parked and went into the building. She and I went into the front entrance and by the main door, sure enough, there was a silver plaque on the wall with her name on it! I remain impressed to this day.

She then told me the words I now live by: "Houston, I want you to work really hard and be very successful someday and always remember that when you work for others you make them rich, but when you work for yourself, you make yourself rich."

This quote rings in my head constantly, and I think about it with everything I do.

She taught me that being my own boss often means that the more hard work you put in, the more your business should grow. That you can run your business in one direction, and if it is not working, you can take it another direction and do something differently. You can choose your own hours and you can choose to partner with someone or get help by hiring employees. And, possibly the most important part - there is no ceiling to how much money you can make. The sky is the limit.

She did admit that there are some drawbacks. For example, the only person who is going to give you a paycheck is yourself. You don't have the level of job security that some may have by working for someone else. However, job security is not guaranteed for those people either, since cutbacks and layoffs are always a possibility. Further, you don't automatically get benefits unless you are willing to pay for them. You must also find your own customers, clients or even shareholders, and continually keep them happy. You likely will not be able to "leave work at the office" as you are at the helm, and at the end of the day, everything falls on your shoulders.

Still, given the choice, I, personally, would rather be an entrepreneur than an employee. I never really liked being bossed around, especially by my teachers, so now I have the perfect excuse to live my life where the only person I answer to is me!

SO REMEMBER: Think of working for yourself and aspire to make yourself rich!

Houston's Interview with his Grandmother, Grandma Linda

HG: "Hi Grandma Linda. For this chapter, I wanted my readers to hear directly from you about working for yourself and making yourself rich. So number one: You have always told me 'When you work for others you make them rich, but when you work for yourself you make yourself rich.' When did you learn this life lesson, and how has it changed your life?"

GL: "Hi Houston. When I was probably nineteen years old, I graduated from high school and I went to college for one year. I came home from college and went out and bought a brand new 1968 Camaro. My dad told me that if I didn't make the payments it would become my mother's car. I immediately looked at the ads in the paper and saw a job in an insurance office, so I went there the very next day, applied, and was hired on the spot. I started working in the insurance business, and when September rolled around, I decided not to go back to college. Instead, I thought I would work for a couple years to make those payments on that Camaro. I learned as much as I could learn. Every time they had a class coming up, I would grab it and learn some more. I learned everything I could in that office and learned to do everyone's job. The four insurance agents that I worked for would go to the bar every day at about 11:30 or 12:00 because that's what they did back in the 60's and the 70's. I watched this for a couple years. I would see them leave for the bar while a couple of other girls and I would do all the work in the office. I came to the realization that we were doing all of the work, and they were reaping all of the benefits. Right then and there, I decided to go and take my test to become an insurance agent and start my own agency, which I did when I was 24 years old. I went down and took my test, pregnant with my first child, and passed with flying colors. I became one of the first female insurance agents in the state of Washington. Later, another way that I saw that I could make myself rich was to become a landlord. I started building buildings, getting duplexes, fourplexes, and apartments. I found out that the rent the tenants paid me would pay my mortgages, my insurance, and my taxes. I learned to be an entrepreneur very early in life."

HG: "Number two: What would you like to share with the readers and listeners specifically regarding working for yourself to make yourself rich?"

GL: "Well it's going to be hard work. You're going to put in more hours because you won't be hitting a time clock at 9:00 A.M. and leaving the job at 5:00 P.M. You'll be working different hours, but the nice thing about it is, you'll be working hours you want to work. You can plan your work around things, like I always planned my work around my children. I was always home to see them off to the bus in the morning, and I was always home in the afternoon when they got off that bus. Any type of activities that were going on I could set my work around. Any kind of dentist or doctor appointments I could always also fit around my work. I worked many nights till after midnight once the kids went to bed, but again, I could choose my own hours, I could choose how hard I wanted to work, and I didn't have to answer to anyone."

HG: "That type of freedom sounds great! So number three: What or who was your biggest influence that led you into entrepreneurship?"

GL: "I would have to say back in the 60's and the 70's there probably wasn't as much encouragement as there is today to become an entrepreneur. I actually just made a decision and did it on my own. I didn't really have anyone encouraging me or mentoring me. I just flat looked at the situation and said, 'Hey, I can do this! I don't have to work for so much an hour. I can start a business. I can be successful.'"

HG: "That's great! So you took action."

GL: "Absolutely. I took action, and I always figured if I failed I could just start again. And if I failed again I would just start over again."

HG: "That's really good advice. So number four: What words of wisdom would you share with the next generation in today's workforce for those interested in going into business for themselves?"

GL: "Seek out people that you can learn from. Listen to what they have to say. If it interests you, take it in. If it doesn't, just put it aside and listen to the next person. Always keep educating yourself. I am still educating myself every day, and I'm still looking at new opportunities every day. I would say the biggest thing is to just learn as much as you can because most of what you learn can be used in any entrepreneurial business. Then all you do is take that business and put some fine points into it. You can learn all the basics of running a business which will works for just about any business."

HG: "I agree. So number five: With you being from the insurance and real estate world, what do you find are similar things in any business that you must do to reach the highest level of success?"

GL: "Absolutely talk about your business to everyone. Word of mouth is the best advertisement. You can pay for all the advertising in the world, but getting good word of mouth among your clients or your customers, it has to start with you. You need to talk about your business, what you want to do, or where you're going and it will all fall in line. If something does not work for you, as I said before, don't give up; keep trying, or if a particular thing didn't work in your business try something new. If you ultimately realize that you need to close that business and start a new one, do it. Don't be afraid because everything that you put into a business you'll be able to put into the next one."

HG: "Noted! Number six: If you could narrow entrepreneurship down to just two words for those considering it for their career what would it be?"

GL: "Start now."

HG: "I like that! The earlier you start the better."

GL: "Absolutely."

HG: "Finally, number seven: If readers and listeners want to learn more, what do you recommend, and where should they go to gather more information on working for themselves to make themselves rich?"

GL: "Well since I'm your grandma, the first thing I would say is pick up Houston's book and read it. Also read other peoples' books, since there's lots of information out there about becoming an entrepreneur. Seek out seminars and gatherings where successful people are willing to share what they have been through. Most of the time, they will share their experiences. They may also share their mistakes and failures so that a new entrepreneur will avoid experiencing those same things. I've often told those starting out, 'Don't do this or don't do that because of this or because of that.' It's very helpful. I've had ups and downs through all the years, and I've learned from my mistakes. If I can share what I learned with other people, they may get ahead even faster by not making some of the same mistakes that I made along the way."

HG: "That's great, Grandma Linda. I want to thank you for your time and sharing all this great advice with everyone who is reading or listening right now and for always being an incredible role model for me."

GL: "You are absolutely welcome."

CHAPTER 17

HEROES

Do you have a hero? Who do you look up to? Who do you admire? Who do you aspire to be like someday?

I have a hero and hope that maybe someday I can be a hero to someone else.

When I was in middle school, one of my classes had an assignment where we had to write a "hero" paper about a "hero" of ours, and why we chose them.

When I was young, my heroes were the same heroes of many little boys - Superman, Batman and G.I. Joe. As I got a little older, my heroes became super popular sports figures. But this assignment made me really sit down and think.

Being a "mature" middle schooler, I didn't want to flippantly name a hero, so it got me thinking. I wasn't truly sure what it was about those sports figures that I admired so much. Yes, they were good athletes and had a cool job, but were they really my heroes? Not this time. This time, somebody was going to have to bring more to the table if I was going to officially make them my hero.

As many of the kids began writing about famous sports figures or celebrities, I decided to try to think of someone who was a good role model, someone who helped others in one way or another, and someone who inspired me to be the best I could be.

And then it hit me. It was not my mom or my dad. It was definitely not my brother. If you read my last chapter, you may have guessed the answer. It was Grandma Linda.

Besides being a very successful businesswoman, she was always making me laugh with her funny stories and hilarious true-life experiences. And boy, did she have my back! I suppose she was always my hero, only now, I realized it!

I did not get a very good grade on this paper because of my grammar and sentence structure. However, my grandma was so honored that I picked her as my hero, that she framed my paper and still has it on her fridge to this day. I even put the essay I wrote about her in my first book, "Schooled for Success."

So I challenge you to think about who might be your hero and why they have earned that position in your eyes. Expand your net. Don't focus only on athletes or celebrities. Maybe it is not even someone in your family. Think about people you truly aspire to be like.

Once you have identified your hero, decide what steps you can do each day to get you closer to being like your hero. What can you do to put a smile on someone's face each day the way your hero may do for you? How can you pay it forward? Maybe paying it forward is just a simple smile, a friendly greeting or a simple hello. You might do a random act of kindness that goes a lot further that you ever would have imagined.

SO REMEMBER: Figure out who your hero is and how you may become a hero in someone else's life.

Houston's Interview with Michelle Anton

HG: "I want to welcome Michelle Anton, television producer and author of the bestselling book *Weekend Entrepreneur: 101 Great*

Ways to Earn Extra Cash. Not only is Michelle a bestselling author, but she was an associate producer on the Oprah Winfrey Show and producer of other major television talk shows. Michelle will be sharing some information about heroes. So Michelle, my first question for you is, can you share with the readers and listeners a little about your success and the heroes that have influenced you?"

MA: "Well as a TV and radio producer, I've worked with some great people. I was Dr. Laura's executive producer for several years and worked with her for five years. I produced the Leeza Show with Leeza Gibbons, and The Montel Williams Show. I've worked with a lot of celebrities like Leonardo DiCaprio, Halle Berry, and Naomi Judd. A lot of the people that I've worked with are on somewhat of a mission. I look at a person like Dr. Laura, who was and still is, an advocate for children, and I really admire people who use their celebrity for more than just being famous, or rich and famous. They use it to help other people. I think that's one of the really nice things, whether you're a celebrity or not, that you can give back and do something that helps other people and not just think about yourself."

HG: "That's amazing! Now my second question for you. Hero is a pretty big word. What does the word mean to you?"

MA: "Well I think it's a person who is courageous, and does what's right versus what's convenient, and they set out to help others. By doing so, a lot of times there are sacrifices that they make. I know a lot of times when I talk to people about being a producer they say, 'Oh wow, you're a TV producer!' It just looks really glamorous and people will ask, 'Why did you get into that?' I can't really say I got into it. I would say producing chose me, and it was the perfect venue for me to be able to help the unsung hero – to help people who didn't have a voice and would not otherwise have the opportunity to speak to millions. So for me it's been more like a vocation versus something that is really glamorous. When you're working, it could be an eighteen hour day. You could be pulling an all-nighter. There's nothing really glamorous about that, but if you're doing something that could be a topic that really helps or empowers, then it's a worthy cause. So, although I've done a lot of shows with celebrities, I'm most proud of the people that I've worked with who have been unsung heroes."

HG: "How can people that are successful or striving for success become a hero to others?"

MA: "First of all, there are a lot of injustices going on in the world. The first thing is to take a stand for what's right. So often, I think that people don't help because they don't want to get involved, or they don't help because they've become apathetic, or they look at their own situation and they think, 'Well look at me - I'm not in a position to help, so why should I? What about me?'"

"Even one voice can make a difference, and I think it's really easy now because we've got so many ways to make a difference. We can vote with our dollars by not buying things that we don't believe are good, or from corporations that may not be good corporate citizens, and we can volunteer. I think volunteering is really important. Even if I only have an hour, that one hour that I can spend volunteering or helping someone will make a really big difference. I think it's just as important to tithe your time as it is to tithe your dollars.

"So if someone is looking at being a hero, I think it's important to realize that no matter *where* you start, you *can* start. There's a beginning to everything. It doesn't matter how small it is. A lot of times people don't start because they say, 'Well, you know, this is so small I'm not going to do that.' They have really big, lofty ideas, but I think you have to prosper where you're planted. Wherever you are, you are in the right place, and it's the right time.

"One of the African proverbs that I really love is 'If you want to go fast, go alone. If you want to go far, go together.' I think there is power in numbers and that it's a perfect opportunity for us to come together and create community and to do great things with other people, not just by ourselves, but with other people."

HG: "Agreed. There is definitely power in numbers! I also wanted to ask you if you have a hero, who would it be, and why?"

MA: "Well, I actually have two heroes. One would be my mom, who passed away a couple years ago. She was the type of person who never took no for an answer, and that's one of the things that I learned from her that's helped me tremendously in life. Another person that is a hero is Rosa Parks. I had the incredible opportunity to have lunch with her at the House of Blues. For people who don't know who Rosa Parks is, she was an African-American civil rights activist who is no longer with us, as she passed away in 2005. The U.S. Congress calls her the First Lady of Civil Rights and the Mother of the Freedom Movement. She's actually the woman a lot of people may know the story of, even if they don't know her name, who refused to sit in the back of the bus and really helped change the rights that African-Americans have in this country. I can really appreciate that because I remember when my mom told me stories of when she was very young. She would speak Spanish when she was in Florida to get into a movie theater or something like that because as a black woman at the time, they would not allow her in certain places. So for me to have met Rosa Parks?! It was incredible, and she is definitely my hero."

HG: "What an unbelievable honor it must have been to have actually met her! That really is amazing that you got to have lunch with such an iconic figure. I am sure you have heard some great hero stories from all the guests and people you have met or booked on the shows you produced. Are there any common traits that you can share that you see with people who tend to be heroes in the world today?"

MA: "Well the heroes that I've worked with are from all walks of life. They don't have a specific thing where I can say all the people that I've met are like this or have this quality, but what I would say for sure that things like education or their social status in life or being from an Ivy league school or anything like that have no bearing whatsoever. Many of the heroes that I've met are considered heroes because they have the ability to decide what it is they want to do, commit to it, and make a difference in a positive way.

"I met a lot of heroes during 9/11, people who made a really big difference. Most of us can remember where we were or what we were doing on that day when we heard what happened. I look at a lot of the people - the survivors, the husbands or wives or parents of some of the people, or those who actually survived the horrific things that happened. The fire department members were incredible, and there were many others who rose to the occasion and tried to help. I just really admire people for saying, 'This is an injustice. I'm not going to stand here and do nothing. I'm going to speak up, and I'm going to make a way for other people who may be in pain.'

"Some of the qualities that I find in heroes would be things like they're fearless, they're collaborative and not competitive, and they give more than they get. Most of them that I've met are very kind. Sometimes, people can be on such a mission to do something that they may not always be kind. It's not that they're not kind; it's just that they're so committed to what they're doing that they don't always stop and think, 'How kind am I being right now?' because they are looking at the big picture and what they want to accomplish.

"Some of the heroes that I've met have had a sense of humor that is totally disarming where you think, 'Gosh, what could I do to help this person?' You are looking at what their mission is in life and what they want to accomplish. You're laughing, although you know you may be dealing with a serious matter, and you know that you have to help them. You know you have to stop what you are doing -- you may have food on the stove, but you know that you've got to turn that food off and help them because their humor is so disarming.

"Heroes are also generous and they're great listeners. A lot of times we don't give enough credit to the power of being a great listener. A lot of the heroes I've met are great listeners because they understand that they cannot communicate with you and get you on board with what they're doing, until they listen to you so that they can figure out how they can get you to be a part of what they're doing.

"Also, I just never stop being in awe of what great connectors the heroes that I've met are. They aren't threatened by introducing you to their inner circle. There are a lot of people that know a lot of important people and they would never, ever, ever consider, 'Wow, I'll introduce you to this person or that person.' Your mom is a great connector. I remember the very first time I met your mother, we hadn't talked for even five minutes and she said, 'Oh my goodness, I know this person, and they're in Florida, and I know you're going to be in Florida . . .' I find that heroes are never threatened by letting you into their inner circle in the upper echelon of people that they know."

HG: "Is there anything else you would like to share with the readers and listeners about being the best they can and becoming a hero to someone today?"

MA: "I would say don't be an accidental hero. A lot of times people will become a hero because something awful happened. What if tomorrow morning we all woke up and said, 'I am going to set an intention to be a hero -- that's what I'm going to do.' Decide to be a hero. Don't wait for something to happen, good or bad, but set it as an intention to help others and to do great things in this world. Don't sit back because you feel like you're powerless, or you feel like you're not going to make a difference to people who don't know you. To me that's called procrastination - that's an excuse. Anyone at any time that wants to make a difference can make a difference. All you have to do is decide."

HG: "That is awesome advice. My final question now is, where can the readers and listeners learn more?"

MA: "I do have a Facebook page for my book. My book is called *Weekend Entrepreneur*, and my Facebook page is 'Weekend Entrepreneur 101.' That's my page where I share inspirational stories and people can contact me or leave me a private message. What I set out to do, my mission, which I started and got really clear on when I worked for the Dr. Laura Show, was helping parents who were either wanting to stay home with their children, or who had a job and did not want their kids to be in daycare. I wanted to come up with a solution to help them create income while they stayed at home with their kids. My mom worked three jobs to send me to private school, and for me to have dance lessons and various things like that. I stayed home with my daughter and was really fortunate I was able to do that. I think for any person who wants to do that, the whole inspiration for me writing my book 'Weekend Entrepreneur,' was to come up with ways that people could monetize their skills or a hobby and cash it in."

HG: "That's great. Thank you again, Michelle, for taking time out of your day to share all of the great advice about heroes for all the readers and listeners."

MA: Well thank you for the invitation. I really appreciate it Houston.

CHAPTER 18

WHAT A QUARTER
CAN DO FOR YOU!

I recently heard a story that I think about every time I see a quarter. I wanted to share this story with you to both inspire you, and make you realize how little you need to get on the road to success.

Once upon a time, there was a man who was down to his last quarter. He went on a job interview at a major corporation for a janitorial position. After nailing the interview, he was asked for his e-mail address and contact information to which he replied, "I'm sorry, I don't have an e-mail address." The job interviewer apologized and said that *he* was sorry, but in order to accept the application, he needed an e-mail address for correspondence and, accordingly, the application could not be accepted.

On his way home, the man encountered a tomato farmer who was selling tomatoes for ten cents each. The man took his last quarter out of his pocket and purchased two tomatoes. He walked a few blocks back towards town, where he displayed the tomatoes for sale for twenty-five cents each. Before long, both tomatoes were sold, and the man had more than doubled his money.

With his two quarters, he went back to the farmer and bought five tomatoes. He then sold those and more than doubled his money again. Over the years, he continued to buy and sell tomatoes and other produce, and expanded his business until he became one of the largest produce distributors in the country.

At one point in his career, he was interviewed about his incredible success. At the end of the interview, the journalist asked him for his e-mail address so that he could send him a copy of the article he was about to write. The man replied, "I'm sorry, I don't have an e-mail address." The journalist was surprised. He said, "Do you know how different your life would be if you had an e-mail address" to which the man replied, "Yes, I do. I'd be a janitor at Microsoft."

PLEASE REMEMBER: Whether this is an urban legend or not, I hope that this story makes you realize that with some initiative and creativity, it doesn't matter where you come from or how little you have to start with. I hope that from now on, you will think differently when you see a quarter.

CHAPTER 19

LIGHTS, CAMERA, ACTION!

I believe that in life, in order to get what you want, you must take initiative. You can't sit around waiting for opportunities to be handed to you on a silver platter. To reiterate what a successful man recently said to me, "If you always do what you've always done, you'll never gain more than you've already got."

So what does that mean? It means taking calculated risks, going after your goals until you've achieved them, and not being afraid to reach out to people or take chances. As the great hockey player Wayne Gretzky once said, "You miss one hundred percent of the shots you don't take."

I always knew that I wanted to make money. I remember a time when I was seven years old and I came upon what I saw as a great opportunity. So what did I do? I took action.

My mom owned a dance studio, and during recitals and performances, she sold concessions and other things like light up roses, glow in the dark necklaces, and other fun novelty items.

I approached my mom and made her an offer she couldn't refuse. I proposed that if I was able to increase her profits that day, would it be okay if I kept the money I made. She laughed and told me to go for it. So I strapped on my blue fanny pack full of change, loaded my little arms with merchandise and hit the ground running. To my mom's amazement, in the first twenty minutes, I made over two hundred dollars and the salesman in me was born! Of course, once I hit middle school, I had to change my look since I realized that blue fanny packs were incredibly uncool.

Over the years, I have continued to identify opportunities enabling me to take action and accomplish my goals whether it be modeling, real estate, private money lending, or writing books.

SO REMEMBER: Always look for opportunities to take action, and make your goals a reality.

CHAPTER 20

L.O.L.

Today I'm going to be talking about L.O.L. – but it's not what you think, laugh out loud. This time it stands for "List of Leads!"

Some of you may be wondering, what exactly is a lead? A lead is a potential customer, or somebody who can connect you with potential customers.

First, figure out your demographic. You need to ask yourself "Who is my customer and why?" For example, my mom's dance studio had a target demographic of mothers with young girls, ages three and up.

Then you need to figure out how to attract those potential customers. You can gather your leads using one or more of the following methods:

1.   Word of mouth – Get people you know, or satisfied clients, to talk to others about your business or venture;

2.   Get similar businesses to share their lead lists, or co-market to their client database;

3.   A more expensive way would be to get your hands on lead lists that may be available for purchase;

4.   Advertise to your demographic– advertising could be a simple as putting flyers out or as expensive as radio and television ads;

5.   Have free giveaways – how many of you have entered to win that free car at the mall? It only "cost you" your e-mail address and phone number, which someone else is likely using for his or her lead list!

When my mom wanted to increase her customer base for her dance studio, she would collect leads by having simple coloring contests where kids would win a free dance class simply for entering. The cost of their entry was nothing. Entering the contest only required their e-mail address and phone number. My mom knew that the classes were already being held, the teacher was already being paid for those classes, and adding another child or two to a class cost her nothing. Meanwhile, the leads were incredibly valuable, and many of those leads turned into paying customers who remained students for years.

Are we starting to see a pattern here folks?

Of course, you can also do more sophisticated social media contests and marketing;

6.   Again, social media can be a very strong asset for targeting your demographic and acquiring leads. It can be simple posts that are forwarded which may go viral, or you can purchase targeted ads to boost your posts;

7.   Online analytics can be a huge help as well, showing you who is clicking on your site, what area of the country or world that those clicks are coming from and more; and

8.   Every time your phone rings, make sure to ask how they heard about you and your venture, and get their contact information.

SO REMEMBER: It can be as simple as a flyer, or as advanced as media marketing – but gather leads, and don't forget to follow up until that new lead turns into a new customer.

Houston's Interview with John Pullum

HG: "I have motivational speaker, corporate entertainer, and television host John Pullum with me. In addition to hosting series such as Discovery Channel's 'Thrill Rides: Put to the Test' and 'More Than Human,' his corporate clients include K-Mart, Morgan Stanley, Nestle, Shell Oil Company, and many more.

HG: "John, L.O.L. can stand for 'Laugh out Loud,' but in the entrepreneurial world it can also mean 'List of Leads.' You are a very successful entrepreneur, speaker, and television personality. Can you share with us the methods you use to get leads for your appearances or clients?"

JP: "Well the methods I have used have evolved through the years. I started out when I was 16 as well in the entertainment business. I would do magic shows and what have you. I have been into this since I was seven and had never really dreamed that I would be doing it for a living, but I'm thrilled that I am. But it has evolved. I have had to find out what works and what doesn't. A lot of people have had to buy lists, because a lot of people sell these lists that are the top people in an area, or the top companies. I found that it does not work well, especially in my business for those types of leads. Every business is different. A lot of my clients are repeat clients or referrals from my current clients. That helps a lot, but it has taken over 25 years in the business to get to that point. I have an e-mail news sign up form on my website and I will also mention my e-mail newsletters. I also have a sign up form on my YouTube videos and other videos. Over the years, I have belonged to a few organizations, and I was able to get leads from their directories.

"Like I said before, as I progress in my business I have used smaller, more qualified, lists versus huge 'Who's Who' lists, which is better for me. I found when calling some of the huge money companies that were on the list that, yes, they were making a ton of money and bringing in a ton, but they were a tiny part of another huge company. So I was sending my stuff over to an office that only had a few people in it that wouldn't have the big corporate parties and conventions and things that I was performing mostly at back then. So it's kind of like a steak company sending out a bunch of coupons to a vegetarian community. It just did not work. To collect the list of leads, I would say put out a good product and offer them something. On my website, I offer corporate party planning tips and give them a reason to raise their hand and ask to be on my list. As far as other leads, without asking them to opt in, just look around. If you are a carpet cleaner just look around and see who you think could use your services. It might not be the one that first jumps right out at you, it might be in another direction. It is all trial and error, and I wish there was a perfect recipe for it. Like I said, throughout the years I have found focusing on a smaller list rather than a huge one is better for me."

HG: "How important do you feel that leads are, and follow up on leads that come into your funnel? And what do you do to ensure the leads are turned into customers?"

JP: "Well follow up is the key. Throughout the years of doing what I do, I used to ask, 'Hey what did you like the best?' It was more of an ego type thing. Now I ask them why they hired me over the other choices they had – why me over other speakers or other entertainers. I know it went over well by the reactions of the audience, so I do not need the little ego boost. I want to know what marketing is working. A lot of people say, 'You called back.' Maybe they called different people, and those people didn't follow up. Following up with leads is huge! Throughout the years I have kept in touch with people through postcards and different mailers. I also keep in touch through e-mails and an e-mail newsletter, postcards, holiday cards, or simply thanking people for being a client or thanking them for being part of my community. Staying on the top of their minds is the main thing. A lot of people only send out mailers once or twice a year. If potential clients do not respond, they take them off the list. You really need to keep in front of these people for quite a while in order to make your point stick. It would be like seeing a Burger King sign or commercial or billboard just once a year. Pretty soon you would forget about them, and you would go into the places that you see all the time. It's the same thing in business. Whether it's the speaking business like I am in, or whatever type of business you are in, if you are not in front of the customer a lot they are not going to remember you when the time comes. It is expensive, but that is why the e-mail list and other things that are very, very low cost like social media fan pages, business pages, and Twitter counts. You really have to keep in touch with people. If you don't do it you're going to lose it."

HG: "Great advice. So, L.OL also can mean "Laugh Out Loud." You are a very entertaining personality. How do you use laughing or making people laugh in your day-to-day business?"

JP: "I have always loved making people laugh. When I was little, I used to do shows in my bedroom for the neighborhood kids -- from magic shows to puppet shows to just joking around. There would always be a knock at my window wanting to know when the next performance was. I never thought in my wildest dreams that I would be doing it for a living and making people laugh for a living. I have traveled to Japan and have done shows all across the U.S., and I still feel like I am the little kid looking out my window making people laugh. But instead of a kid knocking on my window, which would be kind of creepy now, it's companies and VIP clients, or even private home parties, or people hiring for all parties. I am just a funny guy by nature. I am always joking around with people when it is appropriate. A lot of people thank me. This is kind of weird to me. Like when I go to a register at the store and the cashier will say, 'Hi, how are you today?' and I will say 'Well, other than a bad hair day, I am doing great!' and I get all energetic and happy and I am bald and they just crack up. By making people laugh and breaking that little barrier that everyone seems to have, it relaxes them. You get better service, they are nicer to you. There may have been a person that was just grumpy to them two seconds ago and trying to ruin their day, and now you are making them laugh. I have had people say 'thank you,' 'thanks for making me laugh,' 'thanks for making me smile,' 'I haven't done that in a long time,' or 'I needed that.' Even this week a couple of times I went to wash the dishes and grabbed that hose you know on the back of the sink and sprayed myself. I did it twice. I am a slow learner . . .

L.O.L. So here I am in my suit or whatever, and I grabbed the little sprayer for the dishes and instead of grabbing it on the side, I grabbed it by the handle and doused myself just like you would see on America's Home Videos or something. Instead of getting mad, I laughed at myself even though nobody was home. I had a good laugh at my own expense. For somebody that doesn't laugh or is kind of sad, it loosens them up and they can have a good time. Laughter has been part of my life since I was able to walk and talk."

HG: "You are hilarious! I can just picture you spraying yourself with the hose! So, John, what is your secret to success with both forms of L.O.L., 'List of Leads' and 'Laugh out Loud' that you use in business today?"

JP: "I use it and combine it. You never know when your top client is going to close its doors. You really need to keep in touch with everybody. By being friendly with people, I have so many different clients that when they introduce me they say, 'Here is my friend, John Pullum.' They introduce me as their friend. I have known them for a couple of weeks, maybe a month, because they hired me to speak at their event, but I have had that rapport with them. They want to sit me at the table with their family or introduce me to their daughter or their son. By being friendly with clients, by keeping in touch with them as a friend, as much as I send cards and postcard, those do not always lead to hiring me. These people already know what I do. You know, Burger King doesn't have to have a picture of a burger or say come here and buy this. You already know what they sell. So just a card that says "Hey thinking about you guys, hope you are all doing well, this is John Pullum,' they know who I am, and they know how to get a hold of me, or they can look at the return address or whatever. I keep in touch as a friend and it's good to do that. I have had other clients that have moved to other companies and they have called me from the other company. You cannot really focus on one company. I have a friend in the business who would work doing magic at trade shows for this one company for years and years and years and he kind of let the other clients go and did not keep in touch with them year after year. I told him, 'You need to keep in touch with those other clients. They do not know you are there or even still doing this because you are not keeping in touch. You cannot keep your eggs in one basket.' Sure enough, whenever somebody else became in charge, they stopped doing entertainment at these trade shows all across the country. He went from doing hundreds of shows a year to losing that client in one phone call. So keep in touch with clients, whether they go to different jobs or what, because they are your friend and client, and that is the main thing people forget about. You are not just a piece of meat they are going to go after; you are not just a paycheck. You need to keep that relationship going on."

HG: "Do you use the internet or social media for marketing yourself and/or do you use traditional marketing like mail or phone to inquire about leads?"

CB: "Like a high school test, I would circle 'D' -all of the above. I don't use the yellow pages. I saw the yellow pages guy come to my door the other day and drop one off. I put on my shoes and walked the yellow pages back out to his truck and said, 'Please drop it off at somebody else's house.' Everything is online now. Ninety-nine percent of my marketing is online. I use social media like crazy -- that is how we met, on Twitter. I use Facebook. I am kind of liking Twitter more nowadays. I still use my fan page a lot, and I share things off my fan page on my personal page. You kind of have to intertwine them all. I use YouTube and postcard mailings and other unique mailings that are lumpy. Mail that has something in it that is lumpy, like a puzzle piece in it or padlocks or messages in bottles are good. I have sent out a playground ball before to quite a few people. The ball was about a foot around. I would write a note saying, 'Hey your clients will have a ball with my speech or my show' or 'I really had a ball working for you or with you.' The mail carrier delivers that playground ball with first class postage and they usually deliver it by hand, because they do not want it to roll away. That person is walking around with advertisement basically all the way down the street. People are seeing that and saying, 'What is that? That is the coolest thing!' Do anything you can do to stay on the top of people's minds. I have not sent out a promotional packet in five years or so. Everyone books me on line. If they do call, or want more information, I tell them to check out my website. All the videos that are on my promo DVD are online too. I haven't sent those out in a long, long time because nobody is asking for them anymore. I think things are changing, but you still have to send some stuff out by mail because, believe it or not, there are still some people who are not too savvy online, and we all know that. So 'D', all of the above, and you just have to hit them as many times as you can."

HG: "Yes! I liked what you said – 'D all of the above'. With all of your television personality positions over the years, tell us what you did to take advantage of a lead to successfully get you in that position to eventually land the role?"

JP: "I talked about the eggs. Do not put the eggs all in one basket. You know the old saying, 'It is not what you know, but who you know.' Sometimes it is true and it really was with my TV experiences as well. I have taken acting classes, I went to broadcasting school, and I have done some local commercials. It sounds so weird saying this, but I am a nice guy. I like talking to people. I like people. I went to the store yesterday to get two things, and I was in the store over an hour because in every aisle there was somebody I knew who wanted to talk. Luckily I did not buy any frozen items because they would have thawed out. I love dealing with people. I love working with people.

"One of the top acting agencies in town before it closed up, a lot of people could not get signed with them, but I got super friendly with a producer. Her husband actually shot my promotional photos. If you want in with people, it's always good to do business with people who they know and trust. I had heard her husband was a photographer, so he did my photos and I got a connection with her. She started to request that I attend all these auditions, and it just so happened that it was at this top acting and modeling agency in the Detroit area. All my friends in my acting class couldn't get in to these or signed with them. I ended up going to all these auditions, and the people at the front desk started to know me by name, they did not even have to look at the roster. I was friends with all of them. Finally after about the fourth or fifth audition I said, 'So, can I sign up with your agency?' and their jaws dropped. They said, 'You are not with us?' And I go, 'Nope - I have not signed up with you guys yet.' Instantly I was signed up with them. I then did a lot of local television commercials and spots and again, it is just being nice to people. I did not have an ego saying, 'Why didn't you sign me?'

"It was the same thing with the TV shows. Years ago, I met a guy who worked with designing illusions for Michael Jackson with the Jackson Victory tour. He contacted Michael, sent his illusion promo to Michael Jackson who ended up hiring him as his illusion designer and consultant for the Victory tour, and he toured all over the place with Michael Jackson for over 25 years. I had looked up to this guy since I was 16 years old as a magician just starting out. Thinking 'Oh man, this guy is incredible!' So I wrote him a fan letter and said, 'Look, I am just starting out. You are my idol.' It is very similar to what you are doing with Donald Trump and various people. You have to ASK to GET. You have to ask to get, and unless you ask for things, you are never going to get it. Back in that day there was no e-mail so I sent a letter. One day I remember my Dad saying when he got home from work that illusionist to Michael Jackson, Franz Harary from California called, and my jaw hit the floor. I could not believe he had called little John Pullum from Michigan! I just could not believe it! I was nice to him, he was nice to me, and we have become best friends. He still lives in L.A. today, but he was originally from Michigan.

"He was producing a TV show, and he was a co-producer of a show. To make a long story short, I ended up doing a three minute segment for the Discovery Channel. I was very friendly and very nice to all of the producers. A different producer saw my three minute segment and asked the producer of the three minute segment how I was to work with because they liked my look. Franz said I was great and very easy to work with. They called me up and said I didn't have to audition. They told me that they had a new show coming up for Discovery channel and it was a one episode thing. If it works well, they would keep me in mind for this other series; not theme show based, but a whole other series. It turned into over 24 different things with episodes and hosting, and then hosting the series. They credited me with hosting from nothing but being nice and being there and working the way they wanted me to. When I was on the set I was super friendly. A lot of the camera guys were outside, and I would have my own air conditioned trailer, so I would tell them come on in. They were like, 'No, no, no.' There was that unwritten rule that they were lower on the totem pole, and they were not supposed to associate like that with the host or the actor. I said, 'Look, I am just this guy from the Detroit area. I do not have the Hollywood ego, so come on in.' We became friends. I was not trying to get anything out of them. I am still friends with some of them today. We just are friends and it turns into other possibilities for stuff and other doors have opened just by being nice to people. It sounds strange, but just be nice. Don't have that ego. People like dealing with people that they like. That is kind of a long winded simple answer -- just be nice to people."

HG: "I completely agree that you have to ask to get and that you always need to be nice! My final question: Is there anything else you would like to share with readers/listeners to help them reach their level of success, and if they want to learn more how can they reach you?"

JP: "Going off this 'be nice to people' thing again, people like dealing with people they know, like, and trust. I hear it time and time again in marketing. You have to be nice to people. It doesn't matter if they happen to be in an elevator with you or driving your cab. When you start talking to them, they open up to you and you open up. The thing I have noticed with Twitter is I do have an auto responder, and it will send a message to new followers like 'Thank you for the following, I really appreciate it,' or 'How are you? John' In 9 out of 10 people ,their first response to me in a direct message is 'Thank you for following, please follow my fan page too on Facebook, connect with me on LinkedIn, buy my book, hire me, vote for me, me, me, me, me, me.'

"Ninety-nine percent of the people I say, 'Hi, How are you?' will respond "I'm great, thanks for asking.' Maybe 1% say 'I am great, how are you?' And that is HUGE. People are so 'me, me, me' – from their pictures to their fan pages to their Twitter accounts to whatever. People worship themselves. If you could just ask how your clients are and talk to them – say hi, ask how it's going. Do not ask for the sale or anything. And always follow up with people. I always send thank you cards to all my clients. I usually get a picture with them, and then

I send it on the card in a nice box of brownies or whatever with the card. They are thrilled out of their mind to get a thank you card because people do not really do that anymore. Usually people just send an e-mail and it goes somewhere in the spam filter between the King of Nigeria and a widow wanting your bank account number to generic drugs that we are not going to buy. Most people just do not take the time. Here is a great one that has gotten me lots of work . . . if somebody calls and wants me for a speaking event August 15th for example, my daughter's birthday, and I don't get it because they went in a different direction, but I know their big convention is next year again on August 15th, I will send out a schedule reminder on my calendar. I will also send out a thank you card basically saying, 'Thank you so much for considering me, and I am sorry it did not work out. Please keep me in mind for events down the road.' Two things would have happened at that convention - either the speaker would have nailed it and rocked the house and been wonderful, or the speaker would be horrible. In both ways I win because they are thinking now who next year is going to top this guy? Or if he was horrible, how am I going to save face next year because I made a fool out of myself hiring this guy over John Pullum. So when they go to book a speaker for next year, who is on the top of their mind? Odds are the other speaker did not send them a thank you card at all. Perhaps he sent an e-mail, but not a thank you card. They now know I went above and beyond to thank them."

"As far as getting ahold of me, my website is Pullum.com or Funnybaldman.com. There is a lot on there to check out - videos and my speaking information. You can also check out my YouTube Channel. Those links are on my website and you can also follow me on Twitter @JohnPullum."

HG: "That's great! Thank you for taking the time to share all this great advice with my readers and listeners today."

JP: "You're welcome, Houston, and if you are not already, I know you will graduate from high School a millionaire, and have more friends than you would have ever imagined! L.O.L.!!"

\

CHAPTER 21

TAKING RISKS

When I say risks, I am not talking about doing crazy, stupid things that would put you or other people in danger, such as driving down the freeway at ninety miles an hour or jumping off a building.

What I am talking about is strategic, intelligent decisions to maximize money making potential, while at the same time, being downside protected and not betting the farm.

As I indicated earlier, at a young age I was fortunate enough to have accumulated some cash from doing a worldwide commercial. When I was thirteen years old I had the opportunity to invest that money into my first real estate "fix and flip" deal.

I was nervous. What if the house didn't sell? What if it didn't sell for the projected price and I lost my money? All of the "What ifs" were going through my head. But at the end of the day, I felt that the potential reward in this case outweighed the risks, so I went for it. I knew that even if we couldn't flip the house quickly, in the worst case scenario, we could rent the house out until the market improved.

Another risk area for me is in private money lending. Essentially, I am loaning my money to a complete stranger on an investment property. Yes, I put myself in first position to get my money back, but there are other risks to think about – what if they don't make their monthly payments or they don't pay off the loan when their note is due? What if they trash the place? What if I have to foreclose?

These are all risks but, at the same time, I try to minimize these risks by knowing the market so that if they don't pay, I can ultimately foreclose, sell the property and hopefully at least get my initial investment back. I also make sure that the property is insured, and take all of the precautions I can, depending on the scenario.

What if you had $500 sitting idle and planned on saving it for a rainy day but you were given an opportunity to turn that $500 into a lot more. Would you take the risk?

Another example is getting my first book, and even this book, ready for publication. First, I had to enter the book publishing world, a world that I am slowly getting more and more familiar with, but at first I did not know much about. A lot of people procrastinate and never get their writing finished because they are fearful of being rejected by the publisher or the potential audience, and do not have the confidence to realize that their book is ready for publishing. I decided that my goal was to publish books, and I am hoping that all of my readers feel that my books are helpful, inspirational, and were ready for publishing.

SO REMEMBER: When making a decision, do your due diligence, analyze the extent of the risk, and explore if there might be any ways to minimize that risk. Then sleep on it and make an informed, intelligent decision as to whether that risk is worth the potential reward.

ABOUT THE AUTHORS

HOUSTON GUNN, 16, is an author, speaker, private moneylender, and real estate investor. His first book, *Schooled for Success: How I Plan to Graduate High School a Millionaire*, was endorsed by the ultimate entrepreneur, Donald Trump, who said, *"Houston has written a book that should be read by all high school students – and their parents – who are looking for a productive and successful future.* **Schooled for Success** *is a terrific handbook for learning the basics. A job well done!"*

Gunn made his first real estate deal by flipping a property at age 13. This was soon followed by his first private money loan. He then decided to shadow a CEO of a national private money lending company, rather than taking a more predictable approach to a school job shadow assignment. He wanted to spend a day with a successful entrepreneur because entrepreneurship runs in his blood, and he loves it.

Gunn wishes to empower young people, as well as their parents and teachers, to think about the future in new ways. He is inspired to share his ideas and encourage people to ask questions and take risks.

He is launching a new web series "Shooting for Success" with SC Global Media.

Gunn is also a songwriter who plays guitar, bass, mandolin, and fiddle. He lives outside Nashville with his family and enjoys video games and riding dirt bikes with his brother.

SHAUNA SHAPIRO JACKSON is an award winning worldwide producer and distributor of feature films and television. As co-founder and Executive Vice President of The SC Group of Companies (made up of Showcase Entertainment, Showcase For Kids, and SC Global Media), she has produced and/or distributed over two hundred films with talent such as Ben Affleck, Tobey Maguire, John Malkovich, Hilary Swank, Debra Messing, Kiefer Sutherland, Sean Penn, Matt LeBlanc, Colin Firth, Lorraine Bracco, Robert Downey, Jr., and more. She also produced the international hit children's television series "Flight 29 Down," with Discovery Kids that aired on NBC, "Ape Escape" based on the Sony PlayStation Game for NickToons, and "You May Not Kiss the Bride" starring Katharine McPhee, Rob Schneider, Mena Suvari, Dave Annable, and Kathy Bates.

Her worldwide licensees include Columbia/Tristar, Disney/Buena Vista, MGM, New Line, Lionsgate, HBO, Showtime, Sony Pictures Television, Lifetime, Oxygen, Starz, Village Roadshow, Endemol, 20th Century Fox, BBC, BSkyB, TF1, Canal +, RTL, ZDF, Antena 3, Mediaset, NHK Japan/Mico, Disney Channel, Nickelodeon, HBO Latin America, Turner, Cartoon Network, and NBC/Universal.

Shapiro Jackson was previously the co-founder of Curb/Esquire Films (currently Curb Communications) with partners David Jackson and music giant Mike Curb, where she also served as Executive Vice President. In addition, Shapiro Jackson served as Vice President Production and Acquisitions of Curb/Musifilm whose partners included Universal Pictures, and who developed and co-produced the acclaimed "sex, lies and videotape." Shapiro Jackson initially produced several films for RCA/Columbia with Morgan Mason ("sex, lies and videotape"), John Hardy ("Ocean's Eleven," "Erin Brockovich") & Jason Clark ("Ted," "Stuart Little").

Shapiro Jackson is also an entertainment attorney and has written lyrics to several theme and end title credit songs including "Beautiful Stranger," which she co-wrote with American Idol alum and "Smash" star Katharine McPhee.